Images of Man and Death

Images of Man and Death

Philippe Ariès *Translated by Janet Lloyd*

Harvard University Press *Cambridge, Massachusetts, and London, England* • 1985

This book is a translation of *Images de l'homme devant la mort,* copyright © 1983
Editions du Seuil, published by arrangement with Editions du Seuil.

Publication of this book has been supported by the generous provisions of the
Maurice and Lula Bradley Smith Memorial Fund.

Library of Congress cataloging information is on page 272.

Contents

Images of Man and Death

1. The first skeleton *(Homo sapiens neandertalensis)* discovered in La Ferrassie, Dordogne. Photograph taken September 28, 1909.

Introduction
Death and the icon

It is not certain that, as has always been believed, man is the only animal who knows he is mortal. He is, however, certainly the only one to bury his dead. That characteristic in itself distinguishes him from the earlier hominids, some of whom were already familiar with fire and tools. The first man — our Adam, *Homo sapiens,* the Neanderthal hunter-gatherer — was also the first to place his dead in shelters which were collective (no doubt family) burial grounds: our most ancient cemeteries, dating back almost forty thousand years (1).*

From that time onward, the cemetery or the tomb was to be the permanent sign of human habitation, testifying to the continuing relationship between death and culture. This relationship started with burial grounds, then extended to other types of material representation — that is to say, images. Death loves to be represented. That not only was true of the long periods before the invention of writing but remained so thereafter. Despite the body of discourse on death which has flourished ever since the existence of writing and therefore of (initially sacred) literature, the image is still the richest and most direct means that man has of expressing himself, faced with the mystery of the end of life. The image can retain some of the obscure, repressed meanings that the written word filters out. Hence its power to move us so deeply.

When juxtaposed to form a sequence, all the images — be they our own reconstructions of the visible remains of burial grounds, or contemporary iconic creations (pictures, relief carvings, and so on) — could make, as it were, an imaginary, continuous film of a series of historical cultures.

It is just such a record that I shall here attempt to compile, covering the long period of Latin Christianity.

* The arabic numerals in parentheses refer to the black and white photographs; the roman numerals, to the color plates.

2

1. The cemetery and the church

The cemetery
outside the town
Let us pass over many thousands of years and halt the flow of images at the threshold of the Christian era, in a Roman, or Romanized world — a good starting point for our imaginary film. Our first shots will be taken in towns. The model of civilization was, and had for many years been, an urban one. Outside the town, one passed into a kind of semiwilderness in which urns containing ashes were distributed in a fairly disorderly fashion, except where the rural inhabitants had grouped them in patterns inspired by the towns. So it is to the town that we must turn to discover the place of the dead in the culture of the time. What do we find?

In Rome (2) and in Pompeii (4), the dead were excluded from the town. This separation of the dead from the living is the most striking characteristic of these early images. The dead were not to trouble the living or mingle with them. All the same, they were neither banished to some faraway place nor altogether isolated: it was important that one could easily bring them placating offerings or eat and drink close to them. So they were deposited immediately outside the town, at its gates or along the roads leading to it — roads such as the Appian Way in Rome, or beyond the Nocera Gate in Pompeii. The tombs were situated on either side of the highway, constituting two narrow lines of graves stretching out across the countryside.

An alignment, then, rather than a space — nothing resembling our own cemetery. *Coemeterium* is a word that came late from the Greek into Christian Latin, and *sepulcretum* was rarely used. The concept of a

3

4

2. The Appian Way, Rome.

3. Tomb of Cecilia Metella,
Appian Way, Rome.

4. Necropolis outside the
Nocera Gate, Pompeii.

3

special space reserved for burials did not exist: one buried the dead wherever one could, wherever one wanted to, provided it was outside the town.

The tombs whose ruins we visit today were monuments erected by the notables of the town, the *honestiores,* who felt the need to cultivate their fame *(monere)* and ensure that they would be remembered after death by their contemporaries. They built monuments in two places: in the forum in the heart of the town (statues, stelae, commemorative inscriptions), and wherever the dead were buried, in the spots where the monuments would most easily be seen and read by passers-by, along the roads and close to the town gates (3). One left the town by a road lined with great tombs; like the monuments in the forum, the tombs bore witness to the honor of the city.

What of the rest—the humble, the poor, and the slaves? All the evidence suggests that they were buried without ceremony, also outside the town, in a sort of dump. Tombs were thus in effect reserved for benefactors of the city. Municipal patriotism may well, at the time, have been the only force capable of overriding the urge to satisfy ephemeral desires and impressing upon men of the present the contrary idea of a duration longer than the span of life itself—a duration which, thanks to memorials, could extend beyond death.

As early as the first century, representations of death were evoking not so much the mysteries of the beyond as the delights of the present. The skeletons that adorned the drinking vessels and mosaics in the triclinium were not supposed to be frightening; on the contrary, they were an invitation to pleasure, to make the most of life, whose brevity they called to mind: "Know yourself and your mortality" (5).

As a result, the sacred side of death seemed diminished. Typical epitaphs—which, however, we should not take too literally, for they did not exclude other forms of worship of the dead or religions of salvation—all conveyed to the passer-by the same disillusioned or even cynical message: "The hunt, the baths, games, and pleasure—*that* is life."

A change took place in the second and third centuries A.D., one of the great periods of transformation in our cultural history (the next, to my mind, being the eleventh and twelfth centuries). It was in the towns that the cemetery first made its appearance: behind the fine monuments lining the road, humble tombs spread in a disorganized and random fashion over an irregular, bulging space. The practice of cremation no doubt facilitated the irregular manner in which the remains of the dead were deposited. But that irregularity, it seems to me, also had something to do with a cultural feature that persisted even as burial became more common: the body would sometimes be enclosed in a kind of amphora, resembling a large urn for ashes. The protection of the dead was now better assured through the use of stone sarcophagi made of monoliths or masonry, graves covered with peaked roofs of brick (6), and large terracotta amphorae (7).

The dead without rank or fame were now no longer always buried in remote places close to refuse dumps. Some great families left their servants and clients a place after death on the property where they had set up their own monument. Private associations of people would also buy land close to town where they could bury their dead (like the "burial clubs" formed by the poor in recent centuries in Anglo-Saxon countries). The sacred aspect of death, which seemed to have been in retreat in the first centuries B.C. and A.D., regained ground in the third century with the development of a vast religious current of feeling that carried all of civilization along with it and prepared the foundations of Christianity.

The horizontal extension of the cemetery beyond the single file of graves that had preceded it and its use by ordinary folk are signs of a great change in the relationship between the living and the dead. It seems that the humble folk in the big towns won the right to immortality for their dead bodies — that is to say, the right to tombs of their own in the cemetery, where their families could bring offerings and meet together for funeral feasts. Alongside the sarcophagi we often find *mensae* (8), with benches for the feasting guests.

The cemetery now occupied an important place in the collective sensibility of the large towns. And so it was not long before there developed a shortage of space for all those aspiring to immortality, for they were now both more numerous and more demanding. The horizontal cemetery, which had itself taken over from the linear one, was now supplemented by a vertical cemetery where the burial places were arranged one above another on several levels, in simple little cavities *(loculi)* closed by a slab of stone bearing a carved inscription and symbols of immortality. Such are the catacombs of Rome, Ostia, and so on (9, 10). At first, Christians were buried in these cemeteries along with pagans and it is not always easy to identify them. Later, they had their own cemeteries in the same vicinities, and the tombs of their martyrs there became shrines. We shall be returning to this subject, but first we must leave the towns to consider the countryside.

Indeed, beginning with the fourth century, our curiosity as image-hunters is not concentrated solely upon the town and the surrounding neighborhood. For a long time in the countryside, the cremations and subsequently the burials which — in some cases considerably later — replaced them appear to have been carried out in a quite disorderly fashion, with no apparent organization. Soon however, around the fourth century, a new topography emerged, the originality of which is immediately obvious, even if artificially exaggerated by archeological excavations which have uncovered a subsurface structure that was originally underground and therefore invisible. That is what is shown by the photographs of Frénouville (11) and Sézegnin (12). As can immediately be seen, the rural cemetery of the fourth and fifth centuries

6

7

8

6. Amphorae, Catalonia.

7 and 8. Excavations of tombs at Tarragona, Catalonia, showing amphorae and mensae.

9. Colombarium, Vigna Codini, Rome.

10. Catacombs of Ostia.

presents a number of specific characteristics. It is isolated out in the fields, often perched in a high place no doubt long haunted by the gods. The cemetery remains but the village is absent, whether because the latter really was located a great distance away or because it has simply disappeared as a result of being built of less durable materials than the tombs. Today, alone on its acropolis, the cemetery dominates the landscape—a citadel of the dead.

Another striking characteristic is the regularity of the structure. The tombs here are aligned in a particular direction, although their orientation is not constant. At Frénouville part of the necropolis (to the left in the photo) dates from the Gallo-Roman period, and here the tombs lie in a north-south direction. In the later extension of the cemetery (to the right), which is Merovingian, the tombs are, in contrast, positioned east-west. The difference in orientation stands out clearly in the photograph.

A number of attempts have been made to explain the orientation (sun worship, for instance), but they are not convincing. Eventually it was shown that the Christian tombs point toward Jerusalem, the Muslim ones toward Mecca. But more important than the reason is the fact itself, the very principle of orientation. Furthermore, the tombs are arranged in parallel rows. The orientation of the underground tombs was probably not apparent but the rows surely were, thanks to the stelae of wood or stone which once surmounted them but have now disappeared. In a few exceptional cases they have survived *in situ*. "Positivist" archaeologists explain such a layout by noting the replacement of cremation by inhumation, suggesting that inhumation calls for more order in the arrangement of the graves. My own interpretation is different: the space is organized symbolically. The plan of the Frankish cemetery of Rübenach (14), near Coblenz, shows that the regularity of the rows, oriented from northwest to southeast, is interrupted by circular spaces (tombs 51, 46, 37, 47) which are *tumuli*. Here chieftains were buried and they attracted around them, like satellites, a group of other, more modest tombs. These clusters of tombs are also oriented east-west. So the cemetery can be seen as an image of the world: the city of the dead is structured on a grid system similar to that of the Roman urban model. It furthermore reflects the aristocratic organization of the society: military leaders occupy a place of eminence befitting their rank, surrounded by their families and servants. The "linear cemeteries," as they are called by historians, seem to me to be characteristic not only of a particular form of funerary habitat but also of a particular type of culture. For many years, archaeologists have tended to see the influence of Germanic invaders here. In reality, however, the so-called Germanic characteristics can be connected with features of the later Roman world without any clear break in continuity. One is more tempted to see in this type of cemetery a sign of the "ruralization" of society as a whole. The town certainly survived, still a center of life of a more brilliant kind, but it was turned in on itself and the countryside encroached upon it. The linear cemetery is one of the dominant images of a culture no longer as specifically urban as it used to be; in it, the tumuli of the great leaders do not monopolize the entire space as did the tombs of the *honestiores* in the Roman towns of the first and second centuries. Around the eighth century this type of cemetery, too, was to disappear. But it is reasonable to wonder whether it has not survived to the present day in Mediterranean Islam, as is suggested by the aerial

11. Aerial view of Frénouville, Calvados.

12. Burial ground at Sézegnin, canton of Geneva.

13. Merovingian cemetery (sixth and seventh centuries), Vorges, Aisne.

14. Plan of the Frankish cemetery of Rübenach, near Coblenz. From Hermann Ament, *Problèmes de chronologie relative et absolue concernant les cimetières mérovingiens d'entre Loire et Rhin,* 1978.

15. The cemetery of Ispahan (aerial view), Iran.

13

14

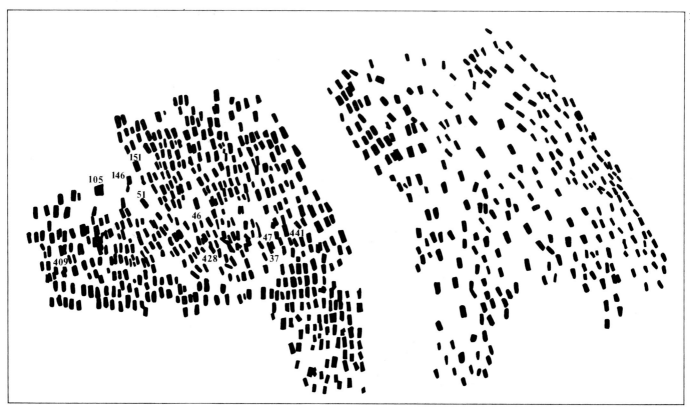

photograph of a contemporary Muslim cemetery (15). The Muslim town of today, with its cemeteries, its baths, and its markets, has reproduced and continued the material civilization of the late Roman period much more closely than Western towns have.

The Frankish cemetery of Rübenach (14) enables one to see how the situation was to develop. The cemetery is divided in two by a blank band in which archaeologists unearthed nothing and which represents

10

16a. Paris in the Late Empire (fourth and fifth centuries).
1. Cathedral
2. Saint-Gervais
3. "Palace" and ramparts
4. Saint-Julien
5. Baths of Cluny
6. Forum
7. Saints-Apôtres (Sainte-Geneviève)
8. Arenas
9. Saint-Victor
10. Notre-Dame-des-Champs
11. Saint-Martin
12. Saint-Marcel
13. Saint-Hippolyte
(Source: P. Périn, Musée Carnavalet, Paris)

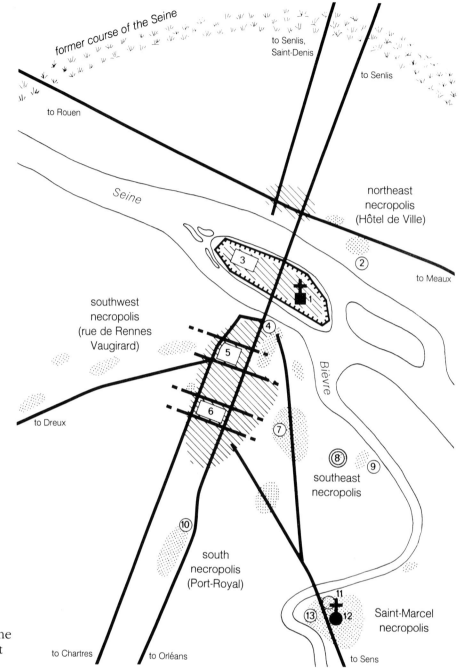

Key to 16a

 Urban zone

 Necropolises

 Attested shrines

 Churches established during the Merovingian period on ancient necropolises

a sunken pathway made by clearing tombs out of the way. On the western side, where the tombs of the leaders are found, the rows are regular. On the eastern side, in contrast, even though the orientation of the tombs persists, their arrangement is irregular. We may interpret this as indicating a later period when regularity was no longer prized and the structural organization of the space had lost its meaning.

The cemetery inside the town

In order to understand what is going on, we must return to the towns and their suburban cemeteries. It is probably here that there gradually emerged the model of the medieval Christian cemetery linked to the church—the model that was used by Western societies until the eighteenth century. That is an anthropological fact of considerable importance.

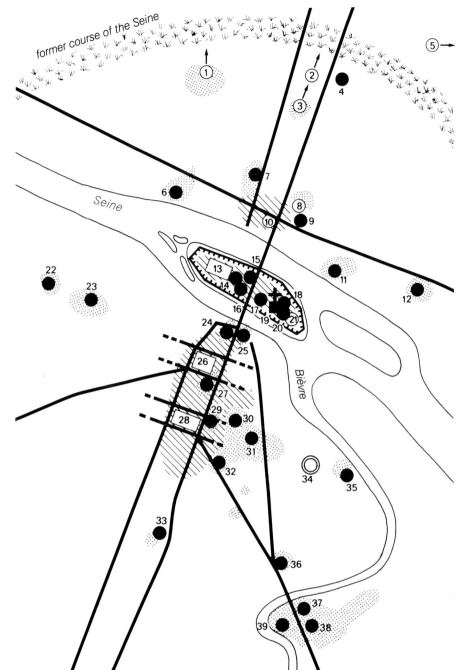

former course of the Seine

Seine

Bièvre

Key to 16b

\\\\\ Urban zone

●○ Known shrines; possibles shrines

░░░ Necropolises

▭
◎ } Surviving Roman monuments

   Let us move to Lutetia (ancient Paris) and consider the distribution of the *extra-muros* necropolises situated along the roads leading to Chartres and to Lyons. Beginning in the late third century, they took advantage of the contraction of the town to expand and move closer (16a). Now let us look at a map of the same site, but at the Merovingian period (16b). We observe that, as Périn writes, "the Île de la Cité had no cemetery on account of its well-defined *intra-muros* situation, in conformity with Roman tradition." This was, in fact, the site of the episcopal group of buildings that comprised two churches and a baptistery.

   In contrast, several churches on the left bank were erected on the sites of necropolises of the Late Empire — for example, at the cemetery of Saint-Marcel and that of Sainte-Geneviève. Nineteenth-century drawings show the excavations in the rue de la Montagne-Sainte-Gene-

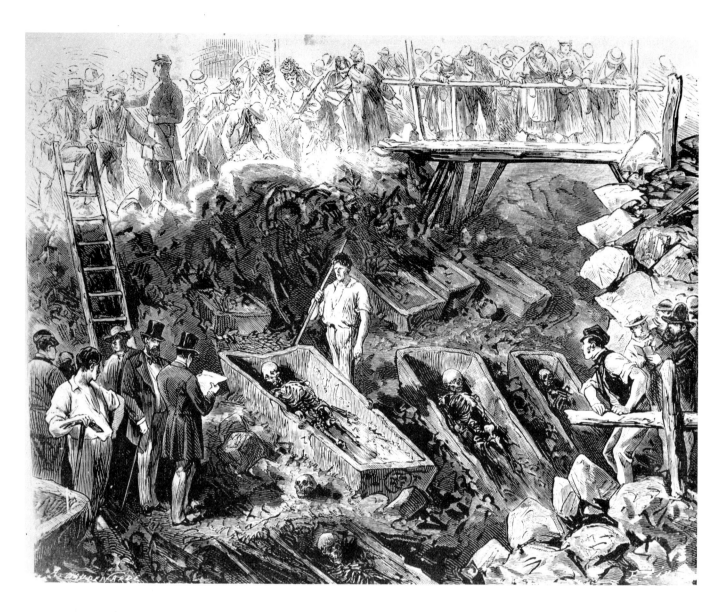

17. Excavations in the rue de la Montagne-Sainte-Geneviève in Paris, in 1873, revealing the Merovingian cemetery of the church of the Saints-Apôtres, later Sainte-Geneviève. Pen-and-ink drawing by Lix after a sketch by Tobb, *Le Monde illustré*. Musée Carnavalet, Paris.

viève and the burial places that they disclosed (17). The same phenomenon recurs in every town of the Roman Empire. Christian saints and martyrs were buried on the edges of the towns in cemeteries used by both Christians and pagans. The tombs of these saints then became shrines; the faithful would flock to visit them and Mass would be celebrated there. The second stage came when a church was constructed on the same spot to welcome and receive the pilgrims and organize the worship of the saints. Finally, in the last stage, these cemetery churches and their adjuncts would in turn become burial grounds sought out by all the faithful who desired to be buried close to the saints, *ad sanctos.*

A new type of cemetery thus made its appearance, still *extra-muros* but now organized around a church. The church then sometimes became the center of a new habitat: the subordinate town or suburb.

Saint-Martin is one of three churches founded on the cemetery of Saint-Marcel and destined to become the parish churches of the town of Saint-Marcel (18). Burial grounds then in turn encroached upon all of these churches, as in the case of Sainte-Geneviève (19). The church was a necropolis within a necropolis.

This is a phenomenon that can be widely observed — in Bordeaux, around Saint-Seurin (20), in Marseilles, around Saint-Victor (22), and elsewhere. Many of these suburban churches were in the charge of large Benedictine communities. Today, the masses of sarcophagi and tombs are hidden by modern urban buildings. But in places where towns of the Late Empire had no successors—for example, at Tipasa, in Africa—the whole accumulation is visible and seems particularly impressive. The apse of the basilica of Sainte-Salsa is surrounded by sarcophagi (21).

An urban model thus became established: the *intra-muros* town with, on the one hand, its episcopal churches and a few other parish churches without cemeteries and, on the other, outside the town, a number of cemetery churches clustered around the tomb of some saint, which became the centers of large necropolises and the seats of powerful abbeys, such as Saint-Germain and Sainte-Geneviève in Paris, Saint-Seurin in Bordeaux, Saint-Victor in Marseilles, and Saint-Sernin in Toulouse. A picture by Hubert Robert shows us the crypt of the basilica of Saint-Denis—the "hole" of the Bourbons, as Madame de Sévigné called it—in a state of abandonment following its violation during the Revolution (23). These abbeys were the central hub of suburbs often populated by the lower classes. The saints' tombs that they contained have continued as shrines to the present day: a nineteenth-century engraving shows worshippers of the time before the relics of Saint Genevieve (24).

Rural areas thus seem to have conformed with the urban model characteristic of the church-cemetery combination.

In some cases the cemetery remained where it was but a church was erected there. An example is Champlieu, excavated by M. Durand, where the church, standing in the middle of a linear cemetery, is itself filled with tombs (25). The same is true of the cemetery of Marville: it has remained in the same place from the early Middle Ages to the present day, set apart from the more recent complex of buildings (26). A church built in the cemetery and consecrated to Saint Hilaire served for many years as a parish church until the end of the thirteenth century, when the inhabitants erected in the town a new parish church, Saint-Nicolas, where no burials took place. The cemetery thus remained on its original site.

More frequently, though, the old cemetery, set apart in the fields or up in the hills, was abandoned in favor of a church erected within the town and of the space that surrounded the new church. At Civeaux, for example, the two necropolises can be seen: the larger one outside the town, now abandoned (27), and the smaller, more concentrated one around the church (28). This was the period (just before the eleventh century) during which the habitat, formerly more mobile and with no church, became established at the site where it was to remain for more than a thousand years, anchored to the church and the churchyard. Cemeteries now became established in the hearts of both cities and villages. The old prohibition that kept the dead at a distance from the city faded away. The dead now entered the town centers. No church was without its cemetery, no cemetery without its church. Indeed, the churches themselves became cemeteries.

The combination of church and cemetery became one of the essential elements of urban and village topography. It can be seen as such on the map of the "seigneurerie et censive de l'abbaye de Saincte-Geneviève" (seigneury and fee farm of the abbey of Saint Genevieve) in Paris, dated about 1640 (29). We can see how the cemetery was built

18. Merovingian cemetery of the church of Saint-Martin, Paris. Drawing shows excavations by Vacquer.

19. Plan of the crypt and burials in the abbey of Sainte-Geneviève, Paris, situated between the church of Saint-Étienne-du-Mont and the cloister of the abbey. Engraving by Albert Lenoir (nineteenth century). Musée Carnavalet, Paris.

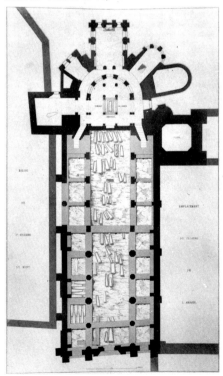

15

20

21

22

into the urban fabric so closely that it is hard to distinguish one from the other. The map shows two, juxtaposed, cemeteries.

One of them, no doubt the older, was called the "Cloistre Ancien" (the Old Cloister). It was also known as the "ancien carré Sainte-Geneviève" (old Saint Genevieve square). On the map, it is covered with short pen-strokes and small rectangles which represent the visible tombs. The whole area was scattered with these tombs, which were, in all probability, extremely old. In 1746 Abbé Lebœuf discovered a great number of them and was surprised at the absence of inscriptions.

The other, more recent cemetery was surrounded by walls — as stipulated by Tridentine law — and it contained three large Calvary crosses of the Breton type. It served as cemetery for the parish of Saint-Étienne-du-Mont. This complicated combination of cemeteries was situated atop or alongside the great *extra-muros* necropolis of the late Roman or Merovingian period which lay beneath the buildings and broke through at surface level in the old cloister of Sainte-Geneviève, where burials were still taking place at the time the map was made (29).

The precinct thus situated at the heart of the *quartier* did not, in this instance, take the rectangular form of a cloister; elsewhere, though, that form was often adopted, giving it the appearance of a closed square like the Spanish *plaza major,* or the Place des Vosges — a square surrounded by arcades. In that case, it was composed of a rectangular courtyard, one side of which was constituted by the church wall, the other three by covered arcades.

20. Church of Saint-Seurin, Bordeaux (excavations of 1910).

21. Apse and necropolis of the basilica of Sainte-Salsa, Tipasa, Algeria.

22. Sarcophagi (fifth and sixth centuries), church of Saint-Victor, Marseille.

23. Hubert Robert, *Violation of the Crypt of Saint-Denis.* Musée Carnavalet, Paris.

The cemetery of Les Innocents, the notorious so-called *mange-chair* (flesh-eater), where countless generations of Parisians were buried, conformed to this model (30). In the fifteenth and sixteenth centuries, the covered galleries which surrounded it constituted the most prestigious area. They were decorated by the famous painting of the *danse macabre,* and every arcade of the covered walk formed a funerary chapel; these were incorporated in the lateral chapels that were added to the side aisles of the churches beginning in the fourteenth century and that were intended either for the tombs of important personages (laymen or clerics) and their families, or for members of professional guilds. The central space was reserved both for tombs (mostly, but not exclusively, of the poor) and for occasional monuments.

There is nothing here to recall the regularity of the Merovingian rows of graves. Tombs that were visible — that is to say, marked out by some sign (a cross, a stela, or a tombstone) — were rare and occupied a very small proportion of the surface area, which was chiefly taken up by large communal graves. These graves were both wide and deep; the corpses would be crowded in and piled on top of one another in layers until there was no more room. Then the overflowing grave would be filled in and another dug nearby. Since only a thin layer of earth covered the graves, the rains and other digging would bring to the surface bones that would lie exposed, providing fuel for vagabonds or objects of meditation for some passing Hamlet.

Alongside the tombs, we also find monuments: Calvary crosses similar to those in the cemetery of Saint-Étienne-du-Mont; large crosses known as *bosannières* because they served as stations in the Palm Sunday procession (this custom is the origin of the connection between Palm Sunday and devotions paid to the dead); pulpits (for in the days when so much of life was lived outdoors, sermons were just as likely to be preached in the cemeteries as in the churches); and rather curious monuments atop which fires would be lit, known as "lanterns for the dead." The fires were supposed to keep away, first, ghosts — that is to say, the unquiet dead; and, second — when the unquiet dead had been confined to purgatory — devils, who took their place in the cemeteries. Finally, there would be other religious monuments which various donors had paid to have erected near their graves.

The cemetery of Les Innocents appears a kind of model for the medieval cemetery: at once a religious precinct and a charnel house.

Monuments like the ones it contains are commonly found preserved elsewhere, two examples being the lanterns of the dead at Antigny (31) and Journet (32), each of which has a desk attached, for the reading of the Passion.

The Marville cemetery contain no lanterns, but it has preserved a number of other monuments of the kinds found in Les Innocents: representations of the Virgin, of saints, and of evangelical scenes such as the *Ecce homo* (33). They probably date from the sixteenth century. Some are if not actually tombs themselves, at least attached to tombs, one example being the image of the Trinity placed between two donors who were to be buried next to the monument (34). Most of these old cemeteries have disappeared, victims of church enlargements or of other construction projects. But some that preserve the form of the cloister, the enclosed space, still survive: the Saint-Maclou precinct in Rouen, Saint-Saturnin cemetery in Blois (37), and the cemetery of Montfort-l'Amaury, which is still in use today (36).

24. Tomb of Saint Genevieve at
Saint-Étienne-du-Mont, Paris.
Engraving by Willemsens-Roland
from *Le Monde illustré,* 1873. Musée
Carnavalet, Paris.

The medieval cemetery was quite different from the modern one. It
was a public and sometimes noisy place with a few random tombstones
and crosses, where people would come together—after attending
mass, for instance. Like the church, with which it was now invariably
associated, the cemetery (or the churchyard, as the cemetery was generally known in England), at the center of the public space, was a
stronghold of social life. The Hellenistic and Roman space reserved for
the dead and for those who brought them offerings, a space set apart
from the dwellings of men, in the Middle Ages became a space common to both the living and the dead, where the presence of the dead
eventually, although not deliberately, became quite discreet. This
promiscuity of living and dead was characteristic of societies of the
Western Latin world. We should imagine the scenes of daily life that
took place there: the faithful listening to the priest ensconced in his
open-air pulpit; the many gatherings to which people were called, such
as military mobilizations and religious processions. Breton legends are
full of cemetery scenes whose protagonists are by no means invariably
ghosts, for the cemetery was also a resting place for the old, a play-
ground for children, and a meeting place for lovers (35, 38). And in-

Overleaf:

25. Plan of the excavations in the
church of Champlieu, Oise. From
Marc Durand, *Le Terroir médiéval de
Champlieu.*

26. Marville and its provostship
(early seventeenth century). Map by
I. W. Jeager, Frankfurt am Main.

27. Necropolis of Civaux, Vienne.

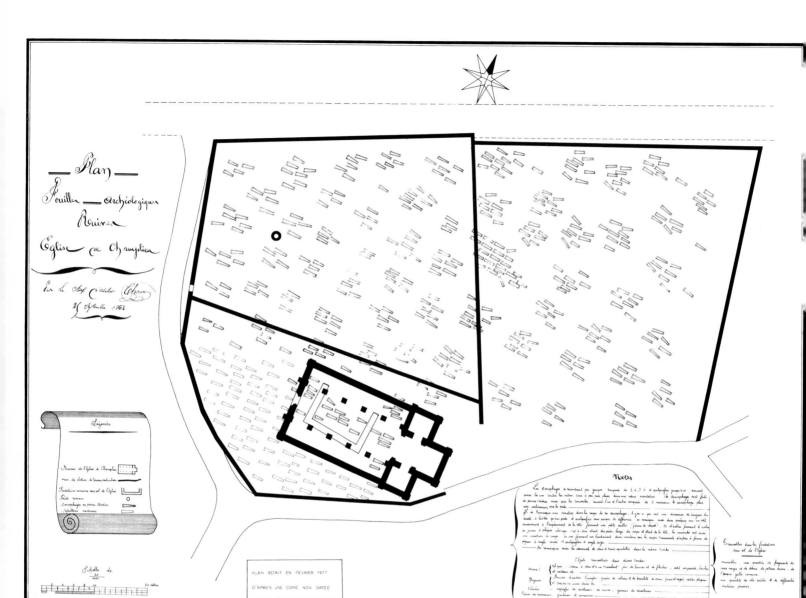

26

deed this is still true of many English country churchyards, which instead of being walled off from the community of the living are crossed by footpaths.

But if the living were so much at home in the medieval cemetery, what became of the dead? On the surface they were hardly visible, apart from a few tombs or scattered bones. Gone were the orderly rows of graves of the late Roman and Merovingian periods. Instead, underground, from which no stelae or other signs of recognition now emerged, the dead were laid out in every direction. Sarcophagi—where they still existed—were sometimes rudely cut in half by the walls of a later church, as at Saint-Pierre in Senlis (39). Bodies were buried one on top of another. The individual nature of the tombs, apparently so strictly respected in the linear cemeteries, disappeared. When an old sarcophagus was reused—a practice, hitherto known only in exceptional cases, that was becoming increasingly common—care was at first taken to place the skulls of earlier occupants carefully to the side of the new one, as can be seen in the photograph of a sarcophagus found in the apse of Saint-Pierre in Senlis (40). But such precautions, and even the use of the sarcophagus itself, were soon abandoned.

28. Necropolis around the church of Civaux, Vienne.

29. Description and representation of the "seigneurerie et censive de l'abbaye de Saincte-Geneviève tant dedans que hors la ville de Paris" (c. 1640). National Archives, Paris.

30. Cemetery of Les Innocents in 1552. Bibliothèque Nationale, Paris.

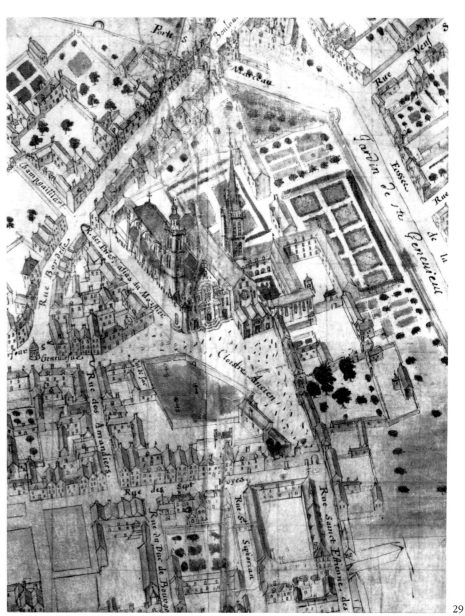

28

29

30

Bodies were now buried directly in the earth, with no coffin, no individual grave, more or less heaped randomly one upon another, as can be seen from the photographs of the excavations at Champlieu (41) and Saint-Pierre in Senlis (42).

Furthermore, these skeletons, unearthed by the modern archaeologist, were not expected to remain forever in their original burial place. At that time people thought it important not to occupy *in aeternum* one fixed, individual spot, but to entrust their bodies to the Church, which could dispose of them as it would so long as it kept them within its consecrated territory and under its protection.

That is why so little importance was attached to the precise place of burial and why the place was seldom marked with a monument or inscription. It is also why there would be no fuss when the Church moved a body from one spot to another. Indeed, around the fifteenth century, the periodic redistribution of bones resulted in a remarkably theatrical décor. To make room for new corpses, the old dry skeletons might be dug up and piled, in bulk, in ossuaries, as in Lanrivain, in Brittany (45). More often, however, the bones would be separated, sorted, and regrouped anatomically: the skulls would be collected on one side, the tibias on another. Each homgeneous pile would be artistically arranged on top of the arcades of the cemetery, which would then be known as a "charnel house" (42). Eventually this term was extended to apply to the cemetery as a whole and came to replace the term "precinct" (*atrium*). The anonymous bones were no longer hidden underground but set on display, exposed to the gaze of the passer-by.

Where the cemetery did not take the form of the cloister, the bones would be collected in a similar fashion and displayed in constructions also known as charnel houses, as in Kergrist-Moëlou, a Breton charnel house dating from the sixteenth century (46).

The octagon of Montmorillon (44) may well have been a charnel house. There are two floors to it; above was a chapel, in which the bones may have been accumulated prior to being dropped through a hole in the floor into a lower chamber, where they would be preserved but no longer visible.

At the end of the period that interests us here, in the seventeenth and eighteenth centuries, the large urban cemetery was a public place casually frequented like a park by the living, and at the same time a place less of burial than of display, presenting a huge exhibition of human bones, some arranged neatly along the walls, others still lying on the ground, thrown up by the overcrowded and newly turned soil.

31. Lantern at Antigny, Vienne.

32. Lantern at Journet, Vienne.

33. Bound Christ (sixteenth century), Marville, Meuse.

34. Funerary monument depicting the Holy Trinity, Marville, Meuse.

35. John Constable, *The Church Porch, East Bergholt* (1810?). Tate Gallery, London.

36. Southern gallery of the ancient charnel house of Montfort-l'Amaury, Yvelines.

37. Gallery at Saint-Saturnin, Blois.

38. William Hogarth, *The Idle 'Prentice at Play in the Church Yard* (1747). British Museum, London.

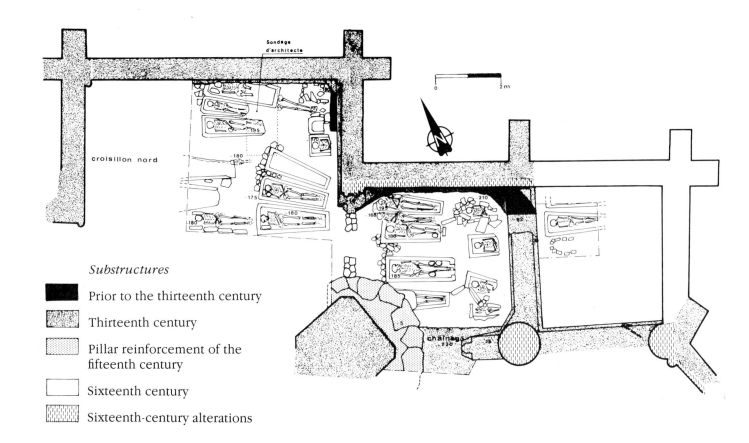

Substructures

■ Prior to the thirteenth century

▨ Thirteenth century

▨ Pillar reinforcement of the fifteenth century

☐ Sixteenth century

▨ Sixteenth-century alterations

39. Excavations of the church of Saint-Pierre, 1978, Senlis. Drawing by Marc Durand.

40. Reuse of Merovingian sarcophagi in the northern apsidal aisle of the church of Saint-Pierre, Senlis.

41. Inhumations of the high Middle Ages in the parish cemetery around the church of Champlieu, Oise.

42. Cemetery of the church of Saint-Pierre, Senlis.

41

42

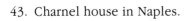

43. Charnel house in Naples.

44. Octagon of Montmorillon, Vienne.

45. Interior of the ossuary of Lanrivain, Côtes-du-Nord.

46. The adjoining reliquary (sixteenth century) of Kergrist-Moëlou, Côtes-du-Nord.

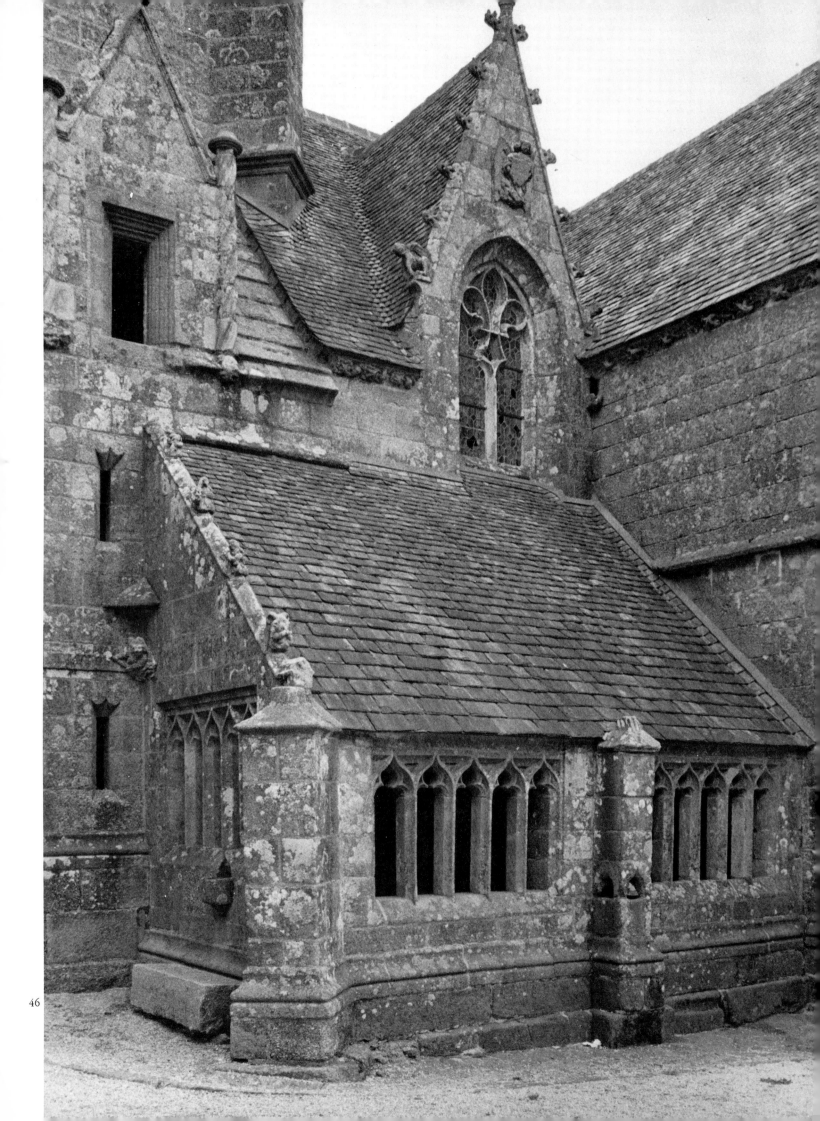

46

NYMHVSAETERNODIVINCTVSMEMBRASOPORE
HICSITVSESTCAELOMENSPIAPERFRVITVR
MENSVIDETASTRAQVIESTVMVLICOMPLICTITVRARVS
CALCAVITRISTESSANCTATIDESTENEBRAS
LETVAPROMERITISVIRTVTISADASTRAVEHEBAT
INTVLERATQVEPITODEBITAIAMAPOLO
IMMORTALISERISNAMMVTALAVDEVICESTI
VIVAXVENTVROSCLORIAPERTOPVLOS
TECOLVITPROPRIVMPROVINCIACVMPARENTEM
OPTABANTVITAMPVBLICAVOTATVAM
EXCEPERETVODVORVMDAMDATAMVNERASVMPTV
PLAVDENTISPOPVLICAVDIPERCVNEOS

CONCILIVMPROCERVMPERITPATRIAAIMAVOCAVIT
SEQVETVODVXITSANCTIVSORELOQVI
PVBLICVSORBATASMODOLVCTVSCONICITVRBIS
CONIVSIQVESEDINTANXIATVRBAPATRES
VTCAPITEREPTOIORPENTIAMEMSRARICSSCVN
VTCREXANIISSOPRINCIPEMAERFTINERS
PARVARIBICONIVNXMAGNISOLACIAIVCTVS
HVNCTVMVIITITVM MAESTASERENADICAT
HAECINDIVDVISEMPERCOMESADDITAIVICRI
VNANEMAMTIBISELVSTRAPEROCTODEDII
DVICISVITAIVITTECVMCOMESANXIALVCEM
AETERNAMSPERANSHANCCVPITESSEBREVI

47

49

50

48

2. Tombs

The next episode in our imaginary film takes us back to the time of the Appian Way tombs, in the first centuries of the Christian era.

Among the other funerary remains that the Roman civilization, like all ancient cultures, has left us is an enormous quantity of inscriptions, running into tens of thousands. This civilization of the written word was, more than others, a civilization of epitaphs.

The common function of all the epitaphs is identification. They give the name of the deceased, the date of his death, and his age (with increasing precision: he lived for so many years, so many months, and so many days). They also celebrate his memory in both worlds: "You will be immortal," declares the widow of Nymfius, and, in a long poem inscribed on stone, she contrasts the body consigned to the dark eternal sleep of the tomb with the celestial light of the stars — the final destination of the soul, or *mens* (47).

Sometimes the tomb bears more than an epitaph: the family survivors may have added a portrait of the deceased. Many of the tombs of the first centuries A.D. consist of portraits designed to perpetuate the features of the deceased, just as the epitaph preserved his identify and, on occasion, his biography.

Sometimes the deceased appears on an upright stela (very common in Italy and Gaul), depicted at work or in the bosom of his family, with his wife, renewing the ritual gesture of marriage — the *dextrarium junctio* (48).

Sometimes the portrait is positioned at the center of the ornamented side wall of a sarcophagus, surrounded by symbolic and decorative iconography. The busts of the deceased may be framed by a shell or a medallion (49).

Sometimes, in the Christian churches of Africa, where the lower level is full of tombs, these are covered not by a tombstone but by a mosaic showing either a simple inscription, like that of Deodatus (50), or else a portrait reminiscent of the famous Coptic ones (51). In the illustration shown here, the deceased is standing in the position of a man at prayer, a very early prefiguration of the recumbent figure found on medieval tombs. At his side is a peacock, a symbol of immortality.

Louis Robert, one of the great historians of antiquity, has called this period "a civilization of epigraphy." But it is also, more specifically, a civilization of the epitaph and the funerary portrait — in other words, a civilization of individual identity. Men retained in death the particular characteristics that had distinguished them in life.

Beginning around the fifth century, the preoccupation with identity after death faded and disappeared. Less and less care was taken to retain any trace of it.

First to go was the funerary portrait, as if the body and, in particular, the face were losing their meaning and quasi-magical force. Over a very long period, lasting about five centuries, it eventually vanished entirely — a truly extraordinary phenomenon.

The disappearance of the portrait can be interpreted only as the result of a deep mental adjustment. Despite claims to the contrary, it cannot be explained by a lack of skill or talent on the part of artisans in a period of decadence. Contemporary sarcophagi (52) bear witness to the mastery of the stonecutters of the fifth century when it came to

From identity to anonymity

47. Inscription on the tomb of Nymfius (fourth century). Musée des Augustins, Toulouse.

48. Lillebonne stela. Musée d'Aquitaine, Bordeaux.

49. Sarcophagus (c. 340). Musée Lapidaire, Arles.

50. Mosaic from Sétif, Algeria.

51. Mosaic from Tabarka, Tunisia.

51

52

53

52. Sarcophagus (fifth century).
Musée des Augustins, Toulouse.

53. Sarcophagus with vine motif.
Musée du Louvre, Paris.

54. Jouarre crypt (seventh century),
Seine-et-Marne.

54

representing not only intertwining patterns of foliage (53) but human figures too. They truly were great artists.

Writing on tombs continued somewhat longer, although it too became less common. Inscriptions became increasingly rare on sarcophagi, whether these were richly decorated like those at Jouarre (54), or plain like those of the church of La Madeleine in Geneva (55). Furthermore, some of the sarcophagi served as cenotaphs. When that was the case, a fairly rare one, the tomb consisted of two sarcophagi, one on top of the other; the lower one, which contained the body, was buried, while the other, visible above ground, was empty and sometimes ornamented, as at Jouarre.

Nevertheless, epitaphs persisted for a long time in special situations —on cenotaphs to saints, for instance, like those at Jouarre, where we find one bearing a fine frieze of shells as well as an inscription, although right next to it a cenotaph to another saint in the same family was left completely bare.

55. Sarcophagi in the church of La Madeleine (sixth century), Geneva.

The five sarcophagi of Jouarre surmounted by their cenotaphs. After a cross-section by Thiercelin, in *Les Cryptes de Jouarre,* Paris, 1974.

Even where the inscription survives, in the seventh century, either the lettering is roughly carved or it is relegated to a position of secondary importance. It has lost its preeminent place in the tomb's aesthetic and religious design, as can be seen from the Ligugé tomb (56). It is the thick, wide cross that predominates, covering the block of stone like a mantle and becoming one with the monument.

The waning significance of the identifying inscription accounts for the fact that even great personages (with the exception of popes, who remained faithful to the written word) dispensed with epigraphic testimony. Charlemagne and his successors preferred, for their burials, the fine sarcophagi of antiquity, which they simply reused, in some cases not even bothering to mark them anew with their personal identity.

Charlemagne's sarcophagus can still be seen in Aix-la-Chapelle, but it is empty: in the fifteenth century the body of the emperor-saint (for he was canonized) was transferred to a sumptuous, gold-worked shrine.

For as long as the sarcophagus continued to be used—until the thirteenth century in some cases, albeit in a slightly different form from the earlier ones—it remained without any identifying inscription. Either it was bare, like those stacked in the *memoria* of Abbé Mellebaude in Poitiers, an ancient crypt of the seventh century which was reputed to be sacred and which for many years continued to attract burials (57); or it was decorated with plant motifs (as at Le Chalard), with a cross (58), or with some other symbol such as an abbot's crozier or the sword of a monk of knightly birth.

In some places the tradition of anonymity thus survived, although, as

56. Inscription (seventh century), Ligugé crypt,
Vienne.

57. *Memoria* of Abbé Mellebaude (seventh century).
Vault of the Dunes, Poitiers.

58. Tomb of Laleu (twelfth century). Musée
d'Orbigny, La Rochelle.

59. Funerary slab at Pézy, Eure-et-Loir.

57

56

58

we shall see, since the twelfth century it had been in retreat among both the clergy and laymen of the upper classes.

Among the masses, it appears to have lasted much longer, right to the end of the eighteenth century when the opposite tendency began to prevail and soon became established. Most people no longer felt the need to mark burial places with a visible sign. The burial place was still considered of great importance — it was stipulated in the last will and testament and mentioned in obituaries — but its visibility was of no concern.

Thus, church crypts were filled with tombs covered by stones that for the most part bore no name. At Pézy (59), only a cross bore witness to the presence of the dead. Elsewhere, during the seventeenth century, priests and stonecutters, in the interests of orderly management, would sometimes number the tombs like plots of land in an official register, but would give them no other identifying mark. Evidence of this can be seen today in the few churches where the flooring remains intact — at Saint-Bavon, in Calvinist Holland, among the Jesuits of Lisbon.

The reign of identity in Roman antiquity was followed in the early Middle Ages by the reign of anonymity, which lasted for many centuries.

The return of the tomb　Around the eleventh century, the long-repressed desire for identity made its reappearance, initially in the form of the most concise of epitaphs (recording a name or a title), later in the more expressive form of an effigy.

An effigy, not a portrait, for a resemblance was not considered worth striving for. However, in giving the deceased a bodily representation, the intention was to provide something more than just a physical resemblance — namely, some idea of the personality. The image of the human body was reinvested with a meaning and power that it had lost centuries earlier: people realized that it, better than any other symbol or sign, could convey consciousness of the self, of an individual's being. It is curious, after so many centuries, to see the rebirth of the effigy based on models which, once adopted and after a little initial hesitancy, remained constant in the Western world until the seventeenth century. To give some idea of this renaissance, I have chosen two examples which could well rank among the most ancient of the effigy-bearing tombs; they are among the first attempts in an emergent genre seeking to meet the new demand for individualism. The subjects are both abbots of great monasteries, one in Conques, the other in Marseilles. The fact is that great lords from both the laity and, in particular, the clergy were assimilated to the saints, who, for their part, had never ceased to have tombs (though unadorned by effigies) which were displayed for the material veneration of pilgrims.

A desire for immortality both on earth and in heaven prompted the successors of the founding saints of great sanctuaries to supplement the inscription with an image of their body, to put themselves on view, since the faithful were anxious to see and to touch them.

A real — albeit nonrealistic — image was now preferred to a symbol or some verbal means of indicating a place of veneration. In Conques, the tomb of Abbé Begon, dating from the twelfth century, displays the representation of a celestial *sacra conversazione* (60): Christ is enthroned in majesty between, on the one hand, Saint Foy, the wonder-working saint and patroness of the monastery, whose grace and miracles had abounded there for centuries and, on the other, Begon himself, newly arrived in paradise and receiving from the hands of an angel his crown as one of the blessed. This is the kingdom of Heaven, and the sacred figures, either standing or enthroned, are portrayed in triumphal attitudes.

This is not a theme that was much followed in funerary iconography, perhaps because it was not considered fitting to place the deceased, even if virtually beatified, on an equal footing with more ancient and illustrious occupants of the court of heaven.

In contrast, the tomb of Abbé Isarn, dating from the beginning of the eleventh century, at Saint-Victor in Marseilles, is an early example of a model that was to become extremely popular and remain so from the Middle Ages to the beginnings of the modern period: he is probably the first of the recumbent figures (61). He lies inside the upturned lid of a sarcophagus, as he may have been laid out for the last absolution just before his burial. But he is not dead, not even asleep; his eyes are wide open, gazing at infinity, and he holds his pastoral staff firmly. Neither dead nor alive, but *beatus,* as his epitaph declares.

In actual fact, he is only half of a recumbent figure, for he has no hands, these being concealed together with the greater part of his body—all but the head and feet—beneath a very large epitaph stone. Now, the hands are the most expressive element of the medieval recumbent figure, more expressive even than the face—a point to which we shall return. Such figures speak above all with their hands, which are of great beauty.

The two cases of Begon and Isarn indicate a change in mentality, a change in the consciousness of the self, although such a consciousness is still very tentative. We will not follow its slow evolution. As in the cinema, we will skip over years and proceed directly to the Musée des Augustins in Toulouse, halting before a fascinating little picture measuring 37 by 47 centimeters, dating from the end of the thirteenth century and intended to be set into the wall of the cathedral in which the canon Aymeric was buried in 1282. Its fascination derives not from its artwork, which is rough though spirited, but from the clarity of its message. It is a miniature tomb: within a tiny space, every inch of which is exploited to the maximum, it offers a recapitulation of the whole of funerary iconography, looking back to the twelfth century and forward to the seventeenth, and of the anthropology that that iconography reveals (63).

Six distinct features are clearly recognizable:

First, the indications of identity and status: the inscription that runs around three of the sides, and, in the two bottom corners, the coats of arms of the deceased, which record his identity using a different code.

Second, the eschatological features:

At the bottom is the recumbent figure with the hood of the canon's cape turned back. Is he dead or resting?

Above the recumbent figure, on the left, an angel is bearing to heaven the soul that the canon has just breathed out. The soul leaves the body of the recumbent figure, which in this case could well be a dead body.

In the center is God the Father, seated in majesty within a mandorla held by two angels. The central space is devoted to heaven, the principal subject of the picture.

Above and to the right of the recumbent figure is a second represen-

60. Tomb of Abbé Begon (twelfth century). Church of Sainte-Foy, Conques, Aveyron.

61. Tomb of Abbé Isarn (eleventh century). Church of Saint-Victor, Marseilles.

62. Epitaph of G. de Saint-Hilaire. Musée des Augustins, Toulouse.

60

61

62

63. Miniature tomb of Canon
Aymeric (late thirteenth century).
Musée des Augustins, Toulouse.

tation of Canon Aymeric. At the bottom he is a recumbent figure; here he is praying on his knees, with hands clasped. He is contemplating God, glorying in God's bliss, but a little to the side — unlike Begon, who was a central figure in his tomb picture.

Each of the elements combined here provided a principal theme for the models that inspired funerary iconography until the seventeenth century. And not simply the elements themselves, but also the way they were arranged; for example, the positioning of the praying figure and the recumbent one, the former set above the latter, is found again at the end of the Middle Ages and in the sixteenth century, both on monumental double-tiered tombs such as that of François I in Saint-Denis and on a whole series of extremely modest wall tombs. Here, on this miniature tomb, the pattern is already sketched out.

The two principal figures of funerary iconography are thus in position: the recumbent figure and the praying one. The relationships between the recumbent and the praying figures, their respective attitudes, and their association or exclusion betray the hesitations of the eschatology and anthropology involved: *Homo totus?* Soul separate from body? Blessed repose, or active participation in the beatific vision? A symbol of man, or a realistic imitation of an irreducible individual, one throughout all eternity? These are some of the great questions posed by the medieval tomb. For it speaks in a language formed by the repetition of the same themes that remained unchanged throughout long series of examples in which the variations, however important, never destroy the unity of the type.

The miniature tomb of Canon Aymeric thus prefigures three great series of tombs:

> tombs featuring an epitaph,
> tombs featuring a recumbent figure,
> tombs featuring a praying figure.

Let us focus our camera upon each type in turn.

The epitaph The epitaph returned in the eleventh century, although in the rare cases of great personages it had never disappeared. The epitaph in illustration 64 provides a good example of these early ventures in the rediscovered epigraphy. It refers to the burial of a companion of Abbé Isarn of Marseilles (see 61) and is engraved upon a reused ancient sarcophagus. It is quite brief: *Hic requiescit arduinus monachus.* There is no indication of age or date. A curious feature is that it is written in an unusual mixture of capital and uncial letters.

Beginning in the eleventh and twelfth centuries and increasing sharply in the sixteenth century, the epitaph became the most common means for men of the Middle Ages to emerge from anonymity and acquire a tomb that was specifically their own. The stone bearing the inscription sometimes lay on the ground like a paving stone or slab. More frequently, however, it was smaller, comparable in size to the miniature tomb of Canon Aymeric and similarly fixed to an interior or exterior church wall. It was not positioned at the gravesite itself, which was nowhere marked and had in many cases been forgotten (62). Such an epitaph could take one of a number of forms. It could be short or long, a simple record of identity or a long biography, an invitation to meditate on death or an appeal for prayer directed to the passing stranger. The effigy-bearing tomb took some time to become widespread and was sometimes rejected for reasons of humility by great

64. Epitaph of the monk Arduin (eleventh century). Church of Saint-Victor, Marseilles.

65

66

65. Polychrome marble slab (1711). Cathedral of Saint-Jean, Valetta, Malta.

66. Bishop's tomb at Elne, Pyrénées-Orientales.

CY GISENT HONNORABLES
PERSONNES IEHAN SANTERRE
ET IACQVELYNE LE CLERC SA
FEMME VIVANS BOVRGEOIS DE
MAGNY LEQVEL SANTERRE
SEROIT DECEDE LE XIXE MAY
MIL VI^C XVII. SOIXANTE ET XVIIIE
ANNEE DE SON AAGE ET LAD^E
LE CLERC LE XIIIIE IO^R DE MARS
AVDIT AN SOIXANTE ET VIIIE
DE SON AAGE

Priez Dieu po^r leurs Ames.

67. Epitaph at Magny-en-Vexin,
Yvelines.

68. Epitaph at Avioth, Meuse.

67

68

SOVBZ CE MARBRE SONT LES CORPS
DE TROIS ENFANTS DV SANG ILLVSTRE
DE MESSIRE IEAN D'ALLAMONT SEIG
DE MALANDRII GOV^R DE MONTMEDII
ET DE MADAME AGNES DE MERODE
LEVRS PERE ET MERE
IEAN FRANCOIS ARNOLD ET MARIE
ERNESTINE QVI DECEDERENT L'AN
DE CONTAGION 1636 AGES DE 2·
3· 4· OV 5 ANS
A PEINE ONT ILS VEV LA VIE QVE
LE CIEL LES A RAVIT LECTEVR NE
LES PLEVRE PAS MAIS ASPIRE A
LEVR FELICITE

69

70

71

69. Epitaph of Pierre Gaicies. Musée des Augustins, Toulouse.

70. Epitaph dated 1745. Church of Les Jacobins, Toulouse.

71. Tomb plaque dated December 14, 1875. Grand Duchy of Luxembourg.

72

73

72. Recumbent figure of Philip I (thirteenth century). Abbey of Saint-Benoît-sur-Loire, Loiret.

73. Recumbent figure of a bishop (late thirteenth century). Gassicourt, Yvelines.

personages (who would make up for this by the beauty of the materials employed, as in the case of the marble tombs of the knights of Malta; see illustration 65). It was the epitaph-bearing tomb that was at first preferred by powerful bishops (66), canons, knights, and eventually also by more modest bourgeois, artisans, and local officers of the law.

Beginning in the sixteenth century, it spread to more popular strata of society. It was adopted by types of people who had never before used it but who were no longer satisfied with an anonymous burial place in a cemetery or even in a church. They too now wanted, if not to be seen, at least to be known through written testimony: this was a period when the ability to write and the practice of reading were spreading (67, 68).

Rural laborers would have epitaphs, as would, in particular, the master craftsmen of the towns. An example is the sixteenth-century master ruddleman (dyer) of Toulouse — who, in a code of his own, expressed his name (Pierre Gaicies), his trade (ruddleman), his canting arms

(depicting a bird, the jay), and the instruments of his trade (69). Another is the cloth-shearer whose epitaph, dated 1745, "for him and his family," is decorated with a pair of scissors (70). This format for the mural epitaph-bearing tomb survived into the early nineteenth century for simple tombs, as in the example in German discovered in a cemetery in the grand duchy of Luxembourg, on which the date of birth is given in the formula of the revolutionary period: year VIII of the French Republic (71).

There was another system of identification available, in addition to simple writing or the ambitious effigy. The later Middle Ages had invented another symbolic language, already put to use by Canon Aymeric: heraldry. Between the end of the Middle Ages and the fifteenth and sixteenth centuries, particularly in Spain and in the Germanic countries, the tomb was sometimes reduced to heraldry alone. A coat of arms took the place of an epitaph, heraldry was substituted for

75a

75a and 75b. Tombstones in church façade. Saint-Génis-des-Fontaines, Pyrénées-Orientales.

76 and 77. Figures of two bishops. Elne, Pyrénées-Orientales.

78. Tombstone of Jean Molinier (fifteenth century). Musée des Augustins, Toulouse.

79. Tombstone (fifteenth century) of J. Lapeyre-Dorliac. Musée des Augustins, Toulouse.

75b

76

77

78

79

writing, and in all probability publicity for the deceased suffered not at all. Where heraldry does not appear in isolation, as is frequently the case in Spain, it is accompanied by other forms of identification of the individual.

The recumbent figure   Despite appearances, the recumbent figure is not (exceptional cases apart) a reclining corpse; rather, it is a stylized standing individual, whose clothing is vertically draped and whose eyes are frequently wide open. He has then been laid on his back, with his head on a cushion. He is in repose. His hands are not arranged according to the artist's caprice but according to a set of rules that makes gesture a key to social status.

The gesture described by the hands may, in some cases, convey the function of the deceased—his "order" in the social hierarchy. Thus, the king holds his scepter (72), the bishop holds his crozier (73) while raising his other hand in blessing, and the knight grasps his sword with both hands (74).

But these poses are neither the most common nor the most enduring. More typical is the gesture of prayer: either the hands of the recumbent figure are crossed on his chest, or they are clasped.

In many cases he is being carried bodily up to heaven by angels (73).

The first images in our collection derive from the model with crossed hands. On the Romanesque façade of Saint-Genis-des-Fontaines (75a) on either side of the portal, we find two such archaic, recumbent figures. This same façade also shows us how epitaphs such as those we have just analyzed, or small funerary pictures of human figures like that of Canon Aymeric of Toulouse, were incorporated into the walls of the church, either outside as in this instance in Catalonia (75b), or, more often, inside.

80a and 80b. Tomb of parish priest Hues (1345). Marville, Meuse.

80b

80a

81

82

81. Tombstone of Dame Marquesia de Linars (thirteenth century). Musée des Augustins, Toulouse.

82. Tombstone of Meheus Duchastelier (fourteenth century). Musée Départemental, Rouen.

Let us continue our survey: at Elne (76), the bishop is being carried off by an incense-bearing angel toward a heaven in which the sun and moon are visible. Compare him with the bishop in illustration 73: he has relinquished the crozier that he would in earlier times have been grasping in his hand, so that he can cross his arms on his chest; he has chosen the gesture of prayer in preference to that of benediction.

Also at Elne is a shrouded recumbent figure (77). Again, two incense-bearing angels are carrying him away to a heaven which, in this instance, is symbolized by the hand of God.

The frequent occurrence of crossed arms no doubt diminished toward the end of the Middle Ages; but the gesture did not disappear entirely, as can be seen from two fifteenth-century flagstones in Toulouse (78, 79). The development of heraldic symbols is noticeable.

The second, and more popular, model of the recumbent figure can in no way be a representation of a dead body. The gesture that characterizes it — the hands are clasped in prayer — removes all ambiguity from its interpretation: such a gesture is not natural to the dead weight of a corpse, but on the contrary demands an effort, a surplus of activity that is not compatible with the inertia of death. So it communicates a secret life to the body, a life that is no longer an earthly one but that of another, faraway land, the land of eternal rest. In Marville, the tomb of the parish priest Hues (80a), dating from the middle of the fourteenth century, is covered with graffiti: one of them (80b) certainly conveys the sentiments of a pilgrim, possibly of the seventeenth century: *Invideo quia quiescunt* (I envy them because they are at rest).

Women's tombs, at first very rare, became increasingly frequent in

49

83

83. Tomb of Bernat de Peguera. Santa María de l'Estany, Catalonia.

84. Tomb of knight Gome Carillo de Ocuña. Cathedral of Sigüenza, New Castille.

84

the fourteenth century, as did children's tombs in the fifteenth and sixteenth centuries. On the Meheus tomb (82) the woman's recumbent figure is being lifted bodily aloft (the body has not been separated from the soul) by angels bearing candles, toward the celestial Jerusalem represented here, as on contemporary stained glass windows, by a crowded design of palaces and churches. Another angel is descending from it, welcoming the dead woman and bringing her a crown of immortality (an interesting contrast with the earlier crowning of Abbé Begon of Conques).

These assumption scenes provide the key to the significance of the recumbent figure: it represents neither a dead nor a living person, but one of the blessed.

Let us now consider the material foundation of these semicelestial figures and how they were displayed. The tombs shown in illustrations 81 and 82 are engraved flagstones that were placed on the ground— not necessarily at the place of burial. Other recumbent figures were engraved not on stone but on brass. In France many of these have disappeared, since the metal was too precious to escape being melted down; in England, however, a large number of brasses have been preserved.

When the recumbent figure was not engraved on stone or brass, with a technique that lent itself to widespread use, it was carved in three dimensions and laid upon either a raised flagstone (83) or a plinth or some other foundation.

The recumbent figure together with its foundation might be set apart by itself (for example, in the choir or in front of an altar, in the cases of the most illustrious personages) or hung upon a wall (a rare practice peculiar to Spain) or, as more frequently happened, situated inside or outside the church in a niche hollowed out in the wall (84).

85. Tomb of Giovanni Arberini (died 1473). Church of Santa Maria sopra Minerva, Rome.

51

86. Tomb of a woman (sixth or seventh century). Vieuxville, province of Liège.

Such an arrangement had important morphological consequences. It left empty spaces above the recumbent figure (the back wall of the niche) and also below it (the visible sides of the foundation), allowing these to carry some illustration.

Beginning in the Renaissance, as a result of the revived interest in antiquity, the plinth sometimes took the form — not an original one — of a sarcophagus, and it even happened that authentic Roman sarcophagi were reused or imitated, to provide a base for the recumbent figure. Generally these bases were decorated with garlands, goats' skulls, rams' heads, and candelabra derived from pagan religious practice. There are even one or two depictions of pagan legends, which were probably invested with Christian meanings. Thus, Giovanni Arberini rests for all eternity above a series of illustrations of the labors of Hercules — doubtless interpreted as an allegory of virtue (85).

The recumbent figure, then, was not a reproduction of a corpse. But it might well have been customary, as early as the beginning of the Middle Ages, for the corpse to be laid out on the bed and arranged in the burial place on the model of the resting recumbent figure.

To grasp this influence of the image on reality, we must turn aside from visible structures and follow the archaeologists underground.

Let us compare a burial place dating from the sixth or seventh century (86) to two others, one dating from the year 1000 (87), the other from the high Middle Ages (88).

In the first tomb, the skeleton's arms lie alongside the body. In other graves of the same period, the arms sometimes meet at the level of the groin. Either position might have resulted naturally as the body was

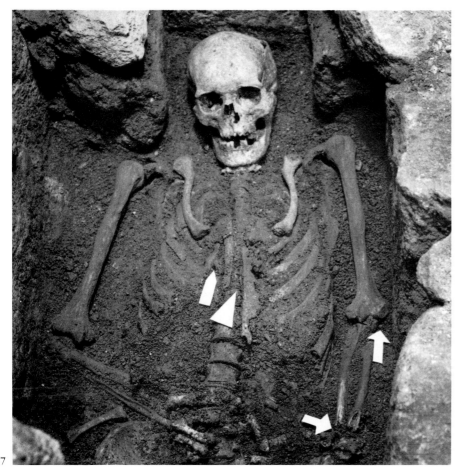

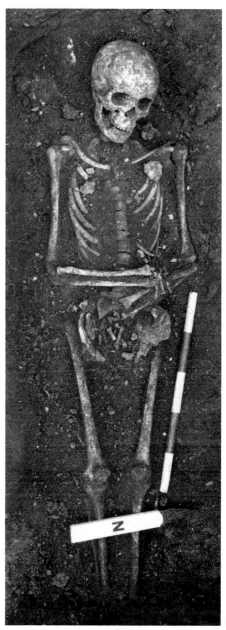

carried to the grave; there was probably no symbolic significance attached to them.

In contrast, the arms of medieval skeletons were no longer left to hang naturally. They were deliberately placed on the chest, crossed one over the other like those of the recumbent tomb figures. In the eighteenth century such recumbent figures disappeared, but the gesture of the crossed hands is common even today, apparently (but only apparently) devoid of any symbolic significance, a survival from a former age and a solution to the problem of what to do with those awkward hands.

What is the importance of this residual gesture that has persisted through the centuries? It does have a meaning, even if it is not clearly and consciously recognized. From the twelfth to the seventeenth century, few of the common people were able — or perhaps even wanted — to have a stone effigy on their tombs. Such a thing remained for many years the monopoly of an elite. Even when, beginning in the fourteenth and fifteenth centuries, the effigy became more common, particularly in towns and villages, it (and even the epitaph, although this was more common) remained exceptional — betokening social promotion. Nevertheless, there has always been one feature common to both the recumbent figure above ground and the corpse buried below: the gesture described by the hands.

The corpse with clasped hands, buried in Church ground, holds the eschatological place of the recumbent figure for those who had neither the means nor the power to produce such a figure, as a double exhibited above ground.

87. Tomb (c. 1000) in the priory of Ganagobie, Alpes-de-Haute-Provence.

88. Tomb at Champlieu, Oise.

89

90

89. Tomb of Carlo Marsuppini (died 1453), by Desiderio da Settignano. Church of Santa Croce, Florence.

90. Tomb of Giuliano Davanzati (died 1444). Church of the Santa Trinità, Florence.

91. Tomb of two monks (fifteenth century), by Matteo Civitali. Oratorio della Madonnina, Lucca, Tuscany.

54

91

At the end of the Middle Ages a number of different developments exerted pressure, unsuccessfully, to alter the eschatological significance of the recumbent figure in its state of bliss. These centrifugal impulses did not succeed in destabilizing it: it constantly returned to a position of equilibrium — namely, a state of repose.

The first of these tendencies, the one that represented the least deviation from the original equilibrium, was toward death.

Let us consider three Italian examples.

In illustration 91 two monks, eyes closed, lie in state side by side upon a couch whose linen coverlet is visible. One of them holds a rosary. At that time, the rosary was an object of piety found throughout the Western Catholic world, even in the most humble of circumstances. At a very early stage it became associated with the laying out of the dead. The corpse descended into the earth with a rosary between its fingers.

The bishop in illustration 90 is also stretched out, but this time inside the upturned lid of his sarcophagus, a reused paleo-Christian one on which the image of the good shepherd is recognizable. He has been laid out for the last rites.

Let us compare his effigy with that of Abbé Isarn of Marseilles (61), which, about three centuries earlier, had been represented in the same position. Despite their separation in time and their artistic and stylistic differences, it is not impossible to compare the two figures. The difference between them is obvious: Isarn is alive, the bishop is not.

In illustration 89 there can be no doubt: the great poet (*magnum . . . vatem*), the humanist who possessed such encyclopedic knowledge, has just passed away. His head has fallen sideways in a

The recumbent figure between death and life

92. Emmanuel de Witte, *The Tomb of William the Silent in the Church of Delft,* detail (1656). Palais des Beaux-Arts, Lille.

movement of relaxation and abandon. The book he has been reading (a profane one, to judge from the inscription) has slipped down but is still clasped against his chest. He, too, like the figures in illustration 90, is laid out on a couch from which droops the sheet that will be wound around the body when it is buried.

All these examples have two features in common.

One is the way in which the body is displayed after death and before burial (see Chapter 3). In Italy, it was displayed on a couch or on a sarcophagus lid. In Holland, it was more usual to lay the body on a bed of straw, in fact on a mat. Artists have emphasized the realism and rustic character of the traditional manner of displaying the corpse. On one seventeenth-century tomb in Delft, a famous and much visited monument, the figure of William the Silent appeared twice, as can be seen in the background of the painting by Emmanuel de Witt (92): first on the left, alive and seen from the back, standing upright in the armor of a military commander; and then on the right, in a nightcap and gown, lying on a bed on a mat of straw. Here is a symbolic record of the customary medieval fashion of laying out a corpse, which is attested by many Flemish funerary flagstones of the fifteenth and sixteenth centuries (Chapter 3).

The other shared feature is the likening of sleep to death and the peaceful expression of the face in repose.

That expression, already suggested in ancient epigraphs, both pagan and Christian, continued to characterize forms of representation in which the subject was no longer always a recumbent figure.

In Westminster Abbey, in the chapel of Saint Edmund, is the effigy of Elizabeth Russell (a godchild of Queen Elizabeth), who died in 1601. She is seated—a posture found elsewhere in England at that date, prompted by the crowding of large crypts. As in some of the reclining effigies (which had replaced recumbent effigies), the head rests on the hand in an attitude of repose or reverie. The inscription on this particular tomb draws attention to the ambiguity of this appearance of sleep. It quotes the words used by Christ when raising the daughter of Jairus from the dead: *Dormit, non est mortua.*

Through this ambiguity surrounding sleep and death, we are brought back to the spirit if not the literal representation of the recumbent figure in a state of bliss—a figure neither dead nor alive.

However, the reality of death sometimes becomes more pressing, in sharp contrast to the attractions of repose.

In such cases, the recumbent figure evokes not the sleep of death but death itself, in a violent and cruel form. The still handsome features of the mortally wounded condottiere Guidarello Guidarelli (93) are marked by suffering. On a wall in the cloister of Santa Maria della Pace, in Rome, we see the corpse of a young man laid out (94); the inscription makes it plain that he did not commit suicide but was killed *(sine sua causa).*

In the fifteenth century, the recumbent figure slips closer to the corpse. It is no longer a body endowed by death with peace and beauty, but a hideous cadaver being destroyed by the forces of decomposition underground—the macabre *transi,* which might literally be translated as "stiff" (95). Later, it moves toward the skeleton, the last stage of *morte secca.* But we shall be returning to this theme in Chapter 3.

The other pull exerted upon the recumbent figure, drawing it out of its original framework of repose, was that of life. The recumbent figure

93. Tomb of Guidarello Guidarelli (1525), by Tulio Lombardo. Academy Gallery, Ravenna.

94. Tomb of a young man. Cloister of Santa Maria della Pace, Rome.

95. Tomb of Cardinal de La Grange (fifteenth century). Musée Lapidaire, Avignon.

D·OPT·MAX·

NON VRBANA QVIES·NEC PROFVIT OPTIMA MATER TOTA NEC EXCLTIS
MORIBVS ACTA DIES·VT NO IMANI PROSTRATVS VVLNERE LAVENS·
DESINERET MEDIVM GVRRERE LVCIS ITER·QVOD SI NEC PIETAS NEC
SE BENEFACTA TVENTVR QIS NAM ERIT IN IDO TVTVS AB HOSTE LOCVS·
LAVRENTIO GERVSINO IVENI CHARISSIMO·QVI CVM ANNOS AGERET
XXXVII·SINE SVA CAVSA INTERFECTVS EST XXIII NVEBRIS M CCCCXGVIII
SANCTA MATER INFOELICISSIMA VNICO FILIO DVLCISSIMO·POS·ET
QVI S CVLTIFERVS ED OSTIARIVS·S·D·AVI AC APTER HOST N FVIT?·

94

95

96. Tomb of *connétable* Pedro
Hernández de Velasco and his wife,
Doña Mencia de Mendoza (died
1492 and 1500). Chapel of the
Connétable, Burgos cathedral.

97. Tomb of Eleanor of Aquitaine
(early thirteenth century).
Fontevrault-l'Abbaye, Maine-et-Loire.

became a reclining living person, engaged in a living occupation, no longer one of the blessed in repose, or a body laid out in death. The original recumbent figures had sometimes been characterized by gestures that, rather than representing an action copied from life, symbolized the quality or status of the deceased. This is certainly true of the tomb of High Constable Hernández de Velasco (96): he is sleeping, his hands resting on his sword. But he remains, even at the end of the fifteenth century, a true recumbent figure in repose.

Perhaps it was the women that were the first to break away from the religious conventions of the recumbent figure. In illustration 97 we see a lady on her couch reading not the erudite book of a humanist but a book of hours. She is holding it propped up so that she can see it. It is striking that one of the earliest funerary representations of a woman should be of a woman reading. Male recumbent figures are not usually

Overleaf:

100. Tomb of Martin Vasquez de l'Arc, known as *El Doncel,* "The Squire" (fifteenth century). Cathedral of Sigüenza, New Castille.

101. Tomb of Monsignor F. de Visdelou, bishop of Léon, by Nicolas de la Colonge (eighteenth century). Former cathedral of Saint-Pol-de-Léon, Finistère. Visdelou is no doubt the person mentioned by Madame de Sévigné in her correspondence, letter 153 (ed. Gérard-Gailly, vol. 1, p. 394).

102. Funerary slab of knight Rudolf von Sachsenhausen (died 1370). Cathedral of Frankfurt am Main.

103. Funerary slab of burgermaster Johann von Holzhausen and his wife, Gudula (died 1393 and 1371). Cathedral of Frankfurt am Main.

98 and 99. Charterhouse of Miraflores (late fifteenth century), Burgos.

101

102

103

104. Tombstone of canon Robert Guériteau (died 1644). Collegiate church of Mantes, Yvelines.

engaged in reading (even if they represent men who did know how to read).

By the end of the fifteenth century, it was no longer unusual to find a tomb shared by two spouses who in former times would have been separated. They lay next to each other, or one above the other.

In the charterhouse of Miraflores, in Burgos, one of the spouses, the wife, is reading a book of hours (98). At that time, at the end of the Middle Ages, the literate woman enjoyed a monopoly over pious reading and consequently also over private prayer. At Miraflores, the husband is not too sure what to do with his hands (99). He has forsaken the traditional gestures of the recumbent figure—praying or holding a sword. He turns his head aside, clasps his cloak; he is restless and obviously alive.

During the late Middle Ages and the Renaissance, the act of reading and the book itself became, for women, a sign of piety and, for certain men, one of intellectual and spiritual activity. In the fifteenth and sixteenth centuries, many of the humble tombs of the Dominicans of the Roman monastery of Minerva bore a representation of the reclining monk, flanked by the candle of faith—of his baptism and absolution—and a closed book, the sign of his sacred knowledge.

As Panofsky has shown, the humanists would create for themselves a funerary mural showing a bust of the scholar surrounded by piles of the books he had either translated or written. Books were sometimes heaped on top of the sarcophagi of holy men renowned for their learning.

But these were brief and ephemeral images.

Longer lasting and of greater significance was the association between the recumbent figure and meditation (100). It is in such circumstances that the model of the recumbent figure propped up on its elbow, in the long-forgotten position favored by Etrusco-Roman tombs, reappears. The tomb of El Doncel, in Sigüenza, provides one example. The deceased is propped up, on his side, although death awaits him; and his page seems already to lament him. He is clad in the armor of a military religious order.

In the sixteenth and seventeenth centuries, this image of the pensive knight leaning on one elbow was succeeded by figures whose expressionist or pathetic attitudes, borrowed from baroque art, were far removed from those of their original silent and meditative forebears. One example is the tomb of Cardinal Richelieu. Another, dating from the late eighteenth century, is the somewhat old-fashioned and rather ridiculous tomb of a bishop of Léon, preserved far away in Brittany. The worthy prelate, dead a full century before his monument was erected, has for a moment raised his eyes from his book and miter, to look at us. No detail of his priestly finery has been overlooked, right down to his scarlet high-heeled shoes (101).

From the fourteenth to the sixteenth century, in Germany, the recumbent figures leave us in no doubt as to their state: they are certainly alive. The stones that bear them were not always laid flat on the ground, but instead might be affixed vertically to a wall. Knights in armor hold their sword, lance, shield, and coat of arms just as they would in combat or at a tournament (102). The women tell their rosaries (103). But even in cases such as these, where realism seems to win out, the gesture of prayer, with hands clasped, does not disappear.

Its persistence through thick and thin is surprising. In my opinion, it

105. Tombstone, Musée de Dijon.

106. Tombstone of Jean and
Madeleine de Sailly (died 1656 and
1660). Sailly, Yvelines.

107

108

109

is testimony to a tenacious attachment to one particular concept of the beyond: expectation, in repose.

That is why, although the recumbent figure became increasingly rare and faced competition from other forms of funerary effigies, it survived in its primitive form as late as the mid-seventeenth century: a standing figure laid flat, with eyes either open or closed and hands joined in prayer, as Canon Robert Guériteau was represented in 1644 in the collegiate church of Mantes (104).

From the fifteenth to the seventeenth century, recumbent figures began to be industrially produced by masons—evidence of the widespread popularity of effigies at a time when candidates for a visible tomb were becoming increasingly numerous. The provincial, legal, and clerical gentry in France were all eager to have their effigy displayed in the church of their own particular seigneury (105, 106). They would place their orders at the workshops of tombstone masons, who would provide a stone with the head left blank. All that was then necessary was to have a local artisan add the head. This would doubtless bear scant resemblance to the subject; but apart from a few, more demanding urban families, who cared about resemblance?

Before its (reluctant and late) disappearance, the recumbent figure lived on as a secondary personage in a celestial scene that, from the fifteenth century on, became the dominant subject for the great vertical wall-mounted tomb. The scene appeared in the space provided by the recess above the principal recumbent figure.

Such a scene had not been wholly absent from the earlier, horizontal tombs of the thirteenth and fourteenth centuries, but formerly it had been indicated only by one or two signs such as the hand of God or, more often, the mansions of the celestial Jerusalem, which appeared above not only the saints of stained glass windows but also the recumbent figures of horizontal tombstones.

In the little model-picture of Canon Aymeric (63), the heavens have opened to reveal God the Father in the majestic attitude in which He would appear on a church tympanum. The popularity of this theme testifies to the power of eschatology over men's imaginations: it inspired the representations of the Last Judgment found in churches, and those of the anticipated joys of heaven found on tombs, as can be seen from illustrations 107, 108, and 109. The recumbent figures are still there, but what are new are the great scenes above them which confer upon them a new significance. First, we find *sacre conversazioni,* majestic sequences of the great saints whom the Church chose to display on its altars (as opposed to the humbler *sancti* of Saint Paul, many of whom were represented as recumbent figures during the Middle Ages and who were now beginning to lose favor). These might be, for example, Saint Peter and Saint Marcel, to whom the church of Cardinal d'Albret in Rome (107) was dedicated, or, on the tomb of Benozzo Federighi (108), the Virgin and Saint Benoist, the patron saint of the bishop, who is seen introducing the bishop with one hand while with the other he points in the direction of paradise. Or the subject might be scenes from the life of Christ, such as the Resurrection (109).

The front of the recumbent figure's foundation, formerly reserved for an inscription or a heraldic device—in other words, for an identification of the deceased—was now encroached upon by other themes: Christ and the woman of Samaria at Jacob's well, or the resurrection of

The praying figure

107. Tomb of cardinal Ludovic d'Albret (died 1465), by Andrea Bregno. Church of Santa Maria d'Aracoeli, Rome.

108. Tomb of bishop Benozzo Federighi (died 1450). Church of the Santa Trinità, Florence.

109. Tomb of Gonzalo de Burgos (died 1509), by Simone de Cologne. Cloister of the cathedral of Burgos.

110. Tomb of Pons de Gontant Biron Chapel of the Château, Biron, Dordogne.

111. Tomb of archdeacon Pedro de Villegas (died 1536). Cathedral of Burgos.

Lazarus (110). The latter was depicted as a scene from one of the Mystery plays: on the left side, the protagonists wait and pray; on the right, Christ raises Lazarus from the tomb.

These processions of saints and evangelical scenes should not be regarded as edifying images designed to move the spectator and encourage his piety. Rather, they are windows on paradise, evoking the uninterrupted spectacle that takes place there for the joy of the blessed. The glorious actions of the life and death of Christ are repeated throughout heavenly eternity like scenes in a liturgical theater.

The surface of the tomb proved too limited to contain such grandiose imagery. The celestial scene consequently tended to spread over the entire upper part of the wall. On a tomb in Burgos dated 1536, the upper part is taken up by an Annunciation and, above that, God the Father is enthroned at the zenith of heaven (111). Normally, this scene would have occupied the back wall of the tomb's recess, which here is taken up by an anecdotal subject, a baptism. The celestial scene has thus been transferred beyond the framework of the tomb itself to a space where it could freely extend. Large or small, the tomb was in the process of full vertical expansion in the fifteenth century, rising toward heaven.

In illustrations 112 and 113, alongside the celestial scene, we find a new figure, differentiated from the recumbent one with which it remained for some time associated. It already had its place in the ency-

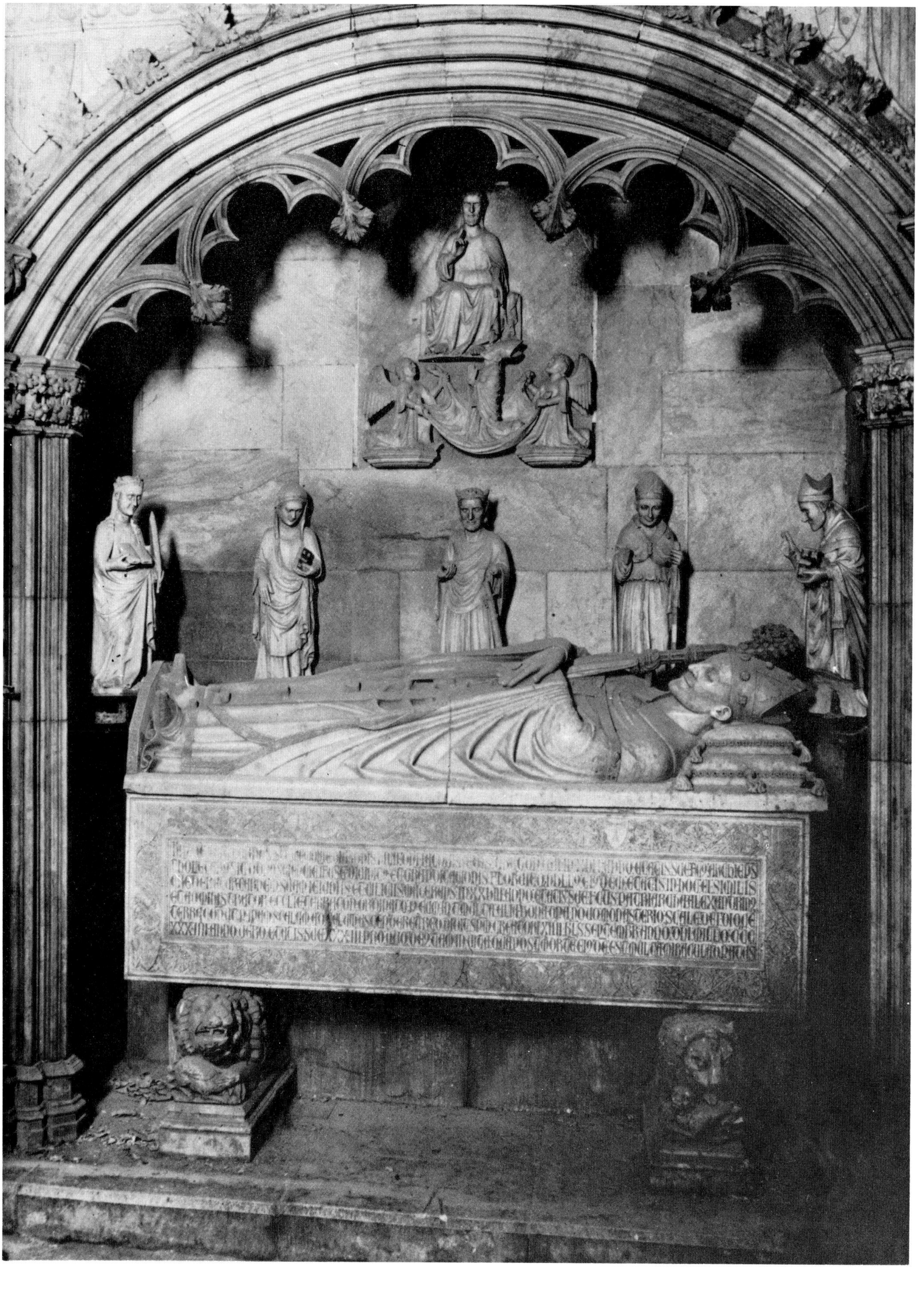

113

112. Tomb of a bishop, Tarragona, Catalonia.

113. Tomb of cardinal Giovanni Diego de Coca (died 1477), by Andrea Bregno. Church of Santa Maria Sopra Minerva, Rome.

clopedic tableau of Canon Aymeric: it is the soul being borne aloft to heaven by an angel.

On the tomb of the bishop of Tarragona (112), the migration of the soul is combined with the representation of heaven, as it was on the design for Canon Aymeric, but now the art is more subtle and, above all, the individualism is more deliberate. At the first level within the tomb recess, we find saints engaged in a *conversazione* (or perhaps they are taking part in the ceremony of the absolution). It is the second level that is of particular interest: here, angels are bearing the mitered soul of the bishop aloft and placing it at the feet of Christ, who gives it his blessing. We are certainly still in heaven, as on the earlier tombs we have considered, but here the center of the composition has shifted: it has moved from heavenly figures and actions to the migration of the soul — a reduced version of the bishop in his little boat.

On another, Roman tomb of 1477, the soul, painted on the back wall of the recess, seems to be emerging from the sculpted recumbent figure (113). This time, without assistance from any angel, it finds itself at the very feet of Christ who has come to welcome it.

The medieval soul of a recumbent figure such as that of the canon

114

115

114. Tomb of Ruiz de la Mota (died 1400). Chapel of the Visitation, Cathedral of Burgos.

115. Tomb with Virgin and Child. Church of San Nicolas, Burgos.

116. Funerary relief by Pierre Saint-André (early sixteenth century). Musée des Augustins, Toulouse.

117. Funerary relief with Crucifixion scene. Marville, Meuse.

118. Fresco depicting the Crucifixion (detail). Church of San Giovenale, Orvieto, Umbria.

116

117

118

119. Tombstone of Enguerrand de Wisquette (died 1468). Palais des Beaux-Arts, Lille.

Aymeric no longer resembled its body. Its form had changed, taking on the almost immaterial aspect of an anonymous, asexual child. In contrast, on the tombs in illustrations 112 and 113 the soul, now separate from the body of the recumbent figure it is abandoning, retains the features of its physical body, but in a miniaturized form. The individual earthly being has not disappeared; it has been reconstituted in the same form. It becomes, in its own right, the figure that we call the praying figure.

The praying figure was to remain the principal one in funerary iconography until the eighteenth century. Eventually, it took the place of the recumbent figure. But from the fourteenth to the sixteenth century, it was often still associated with the latter, which remained stretched out on the plinth at the first level of the tomb. On some tombs, the praying figure kneels before the celestial scene that occupies the second level of the tomb—a Madonna della Misericordia (114), offering shelter beneath her cloak, as if beneath wings *(sub umbra alarum),* to those seeking her protection, or a Virgin with Child (115), as the case may be.

This positioning of the praying figure above the recumbent one testifies to the belief in the duality of existence, a belief that was accepted at the time by a largely ecclesiastical elite, under the influence of either scholasticism or Platonism. Dualism posited an opposition between the perishable body and the immortal soul. In contrast, most of the lesser notables, who aimed, thanks to a visible tomb, to emerge from the anonymity of burial, were obstinately and deeply set against this concept. They would favor *either* a praying *or* a recumbent figure, but never both at once. That is why traditional tombs of recumbent figures remained in use for many years, until the mid-seventeenth century, and why, at the same time, the recumbent figure of the lower level of the two-tiered aristocratic tomb no longer had any *raison d'être,* given that it was reduced to a body without a soul. The praying figure was left on its own. The tomb with a praying figure, nearly always a mural (in contrast to the tomb with a recumbent figure), thus returned to the original format comprising a single level. It consisted of three elements: the epitaph, the praying figure (in many cases accompanied by his patron saint), and the religious scene, which until the fifteenth century took up most of the space. *The recumbent figure had disappeared.*

Such a model suited not only works of a refined artistic quality (116), but also smaller tableaux that were both more clumsy and more common (117). That is why it was adopted in the fifteenth and sixteenth centuries by a rapidly expanding social category—the gentry, legal magistrates, town bourgeois—and, in the seventeenth century, even by prosperous laborers or master craftsmen such as those of Marville. These tableaux, executed in stone or brass or sometimes in paint (118), would cover the church walls and pillars; a few examples still survive.

Finally, one other feature appears: the deceased is accompanied by his wife—in many cases by a succession of wives (remarriages were frequent)—and by his children too: father and sons on the left, mother and daughters on the right (119). This iconography testifies to the development of a modern family attachment in certain milieus of the new society of the Ancien Régime. The tomb became a family portrait, whose funerary purpose was less and less evident. It is not limited to the dead: living children appear in order of age. However, on the painted tombs that are frequent in Germanic and Scandinavian countries, the effigies of children who predeceased their parents bear a distinguishing mark—a little red cross on their heads, for example; and in English tomb sculpture they carry skulls (or, in the case of infants, rest their heads upon them). To arrive at this classical family portrait, all that was necessary was to suppress the celestial scene.

It was a model that corresponded to the sensibility of the age, for it became common not only in churches but also in open-air cemeteries, where the humbler occupants were beginning to cultivate their memorials by means of visible and durable signs comparable to those that already filled the sanctuaries. Most of these monuments have been destroyed. But some still survive near Marville, in a very ancient cemetery possibly dating from the late Middle Ages and still in use today. In the 1870s, a parish priest and a mayor had the happy thought of preserving the finest of the tombs by placing them in an abandoned twelfth-century church, which thus became a marvelous museum of popular funerary art of the seventeenth century. Now, what impression do these tombs make on us? Some have remained *in situ.* It is just as if the tableau with praying figure had been removed from the interior church wall and set up outdoors, in the cemetery. When thus transported, the tableau of indoors took the form of a stela such as can still be found in English and American churchyards. The headstone decorations of the

Overleaf:

121. Tomb of knight Jehan Saint-André (died 1525). Musée des Augustins, Toulouse.

122. Praying figure and epitaph. Winchester, England.

123. Fragments from the mausoleum of the duc de Villeroy (seventeenth century). Magny-en-Vexin, Yvelines.

124. Tomb of the Infante Alonso (died 1470), brother of Isabelle the Catholic, by Gil de Siloé. Charterhouse of Miraflores, Burgos.

120. Headstone of Thomas Edmonds (1756). Parish church, Hungars, Virginia. On the tombs and cemeteries of Virginia, see Patrick Henry Butler, "On the Memorial Art of Tidewater Virginia" (Dissertation, Johns Hopkins University, 1969).

121

122

ELLEONORA IACET CONIVX MEA CHARA SVB ISTO
MARMORE: NI CHARAM FLEVERO, MARMOR. ERO
FÆMINA MVLTIPLICI VIRTVTIS AMORE DECORA
I LLECEBRASQ. SOLI SPREVIT, AMORE POLI
SANCTA FVIT, SANCTE VIXIT SANCTEQ RECESSIT
IN CÆLO TANDEM SANCTIOR ILLA MANET.

T:S: MARITVS DEFLEVIT

123

125. Tomb of the Bolognetti family (1675). Church of Gesù e Maria, Rome.

126. Tomb of Maria Colomba Vicentini (1725), by Bernardino Cametti. Church of San Marcello, Rome.

seventeenth to the early nineteenth century derive from medieval iconography: the little winged head with which they are crowned no doubt stems from the angel of paradise or from the soul in scenes of assumption — in short, from the religious scene of mural funerary iconography (120).

There can be little doubt that the praying figures in tomb sculpture are no longer of this world but already belong to the next. This becomes particularly clear when we study those altarpieces from Italian churches of the fourteenth, fifteenth, and sixteenth centuries which originally adorned family burial chapels. In these altarpieces the founder of the chapel would be represented, often with his wife and with junior members of his family, kneeling before the Virgin and Child to whom they are presented by the patron saints of the church, or by their family, or by their name-saints (even when they do not appear in person, these saints may still be considered as interceding for them at the court of heaven). At first, the kneeling founders were given smaller stature, and were painted in profile and placed to the side; but when art became more naturalistic, space replaced scale as the means of discrimination: they came to occupy a separate, lower area nearer the viewer. In all cases, however, they were in the presence of the divinity.

Although the praying figure in such scenes is indeed a saint in heaven, he has not yet reached the heaven of the greatest saints. He awaits his admission to paradise in a kind of antechamber (symbolized, in the early tableaux, by his size and position). This waiting-chamber is not a place of purification, despite the fact that this was the time of indulgences and devotions performed for souls in purgatory. Purgatory does not figure on the tombs. Each man would certainly make provision in his will for services and prayers to be directed to his salvation, but he did not expect his place to be anywhere other than in heaven. He nevertheless had the humility not to push himself forward to the first

127. Recumbent figure of Robert the Pious (died 1031). Abbey church of Saint-Denis.

rank but kept his distance a little, in an attitude of reserve that did not appear to be totally definitive: the expectation of the praying figure seems to me to echo the repose of the recumbent figure, although perhaps with slightly more ambiguity.

Let us look once again at the tomb of Canon Aymeric (63), dated 1282; the migration of the soul and the recumbent figure, its main elements, eventually both disappeared in the art of later periods. In the seventeenth century, it was the turn of the large devotional scene to go. First it was contracted: on the tomb in illustration 121 it is reduced to the face of God, half hidden in the decorative foliage. Then it disappeared completely and the praying figure took up all the space of the recess, whether portrayed simply and starkly in the earlier style, as in England (122), or laden with flamboyant decoration, as in Spain (124). It thus changed from a miniature representation of the subject to one that was life-size or even larger. In its last stage, in the seventeenth century, it became detached from the wall and took the form of a free-standing statue that could be placed wherever desired in the church.

In most surviving examples, the figure kneels before and sometimes leans against a sort of prayer table, which during that period acquired the charming name of *prie-Dieu* (or *prié-Dieu*). This piece of furniture soon became very popular, for it provided comfort during prayer (which was now of a more individual nature), either in the family chapel where milord would attend Sunday mass, or in a private oratory at home, or simply in one's own room, which also became a place of prayer. The French praying figure is more or less static in its devotions (123). On further consideration, we realize that the traditional religious scene did not really disappear: it simply became invisible, within the figure's personal meditation.

In contrast, the Italian praying figure, as illustrated by examples in Rome sculpted by Bernini or his followers, does not remain still or even in a kneeling position: it is animated, abandoning itself to an ardor approaching ecstasy.

Consider the Bolognetti (125) in their church of Gesù e Maria on the Corso, a church which they turned into a great family tomb. There are Bolognetti everywhere. Some are represented in their private *loggia* on the upper level, as if in a theater, leaning forward toward the altar. This enraptured pose is found elsewhere, too — in San Marcello, for example (126). The Bolognetti have set their missals on a cushioned marble balustrade, which serves them as a *prie-Dieu.* They are speaking together with great emotion, deeply moved by the whole spectacle. It is, in truth, a double spectacle: as living people, they are attending their parish Mass; as members of the blessed, they are in paradise contemplating the mystic altar — the *sublime altare* — of the canon of Roman liturgy, to which angels are bringing consecrated offerings from all the altars on earth.

The great tomb statues of the seventeenth century are the last in an uninterrupted series stretching over half a millenium that began with the recumbent figures of the twelfth century and continued to the praying figures of the seventeenth. In the eighteenth century came a hiatus, marked by iconographic hesitations. It was not until the nineteenth century that a new stable funerary model appeared in the cemeteries — one which bore no relation to the developments that had begun in the Middle Ages.

As one considers the long sequence of effigy-bearing tombs, it is impossible not to be struck by the increasing verisimilitude of the images.

The earliest effigies were ideal or "idealized" portraits (A. Erlande-Brandenburg) which did not aim at any resemblance. When Saint Louis undertook to restore the recumbent figures of his predecessors in Saint-Denis—that of Robert the Pious, for instance (127)—he was concerned only to give them features and attitudes that corresponded to their royal function. However, the craftsmen who sculpted the tombs, anxious that the figures should not look too much alike, made them distinguishable by giving them invented physical characteristics, thus producing portraits that were not only ideal but imaginary.

Until the seventeenth century, the craftsmen who supplied half-finished tombstones to be sold to minor notables were even less concerned with resemblance. Their clientele required only that the costume, for example, should clearly reflect the status of the deceased and that there should be some detail or other to indicate his right to eternal blessedness.

Among the elite, this indifference disappeared earlier, in the fifteenth century. It was no accident that a desire for resemblance coincided with the appearance of the praying figure, the goal in both cases being greater individualization. The first portraits to be resemblances were the praying figures on tombs. Later, as we have seen, the praying figure lost its funerary function and became a portrait pure and simple, either grouped with a religious scene (for example, Jean Fouquet's

128. Recumbent figures of Jean sans Peur (died 1419), and his wife, Marguerite de Bavière. Musée des Beaux-Arts, Dijon.

129

130

131

129. Recumbent figures of Charles III, "the Noble," king of Navarre (died 1425), and his wife, Eleanora of Castille (died 1416), by Janin l'Home. Cathedral of Pamplona, Navarre.

130. Funerary mask (early fourteenth century). Former abbey of Saint-Vaast, Arras.

131. Funerary portrait (early fourteenth century). Musée des Augustins, Toulouse.

132. Recumbent figure. Musée des Augustins, Toulouse.

132

133

134

D · V

DOMINICVS·BERTINVS
LVCEN·LATERANEN·ETCE
SARTE·AVIARVM·COMES
AC·SCE·APL·SEDIS·SECNA
RIVS·TABERNACVLO·SALV
ATORIS·INSIGNI·OPERE·FR
SVO·PROPIVS·EXCITATO·BI
BI·E·SVEVE·R·SALVE·CONR··
SVE·INCOMPARABILI·EORV·O
POSERIS·VIVVS·DICAVIT·SACR·
·SALVTIS·ANNO·
·M·CCCCLXXVIIII·

133. Tomb of Giovanni Girolamo
Albani. Church of Santa Maria del
Popolo, Rome.

134. Tomb of Domenico Bertini
(fifteenth century), by Matteo
Civitali. Cathedral of Lucca, Tuscany.

Guillaume des Ursins, or Van Eyck's knight Rollin) or on its own (in the case of Jean the Good, or the duke and duchess of Urbino). At first, it would be presented in profile or in a three-quarter view.

In the seventeenth century, some portraits intended for the home were still inspired by the model of the praying figure kneeling before a religious scene.

In a letter dated 30 January 1652, Guy Patin describes his "study" as follows: "I have had placed on the mantlepiece a fine painting of a crucifix which a painter . . . gave me in 1627. We are both there, on either side of the Lord, as master and mistress" (cited by Jean-Claude Margolin). The text is not altogether clear. Either the married couple appeared in the painting of Christ, or—as seems more likely— Guy Patin had arranged three pictures in such a way as to create that impression.

However, if the praying figure continued for a long time to be used as a portrait in the home, it did not have a monopoly over resemblance. The recumbent figure, though confined to its funerary role, also sought and achieved it.

According to A. Erlande-Brandenburg, the first realistic royal recumbent figure is that of Charles VI, which was executed during the king's lifetime.

In the absence of such foresight, scrupulous craftsmen would have had to work from a drawing of the deceased or from a plaster cast of his face made on his deathbed. The tomb was now used to display in a lasting fashion the subject's features as recorded at the moment of death. The practice gave rise to many admirable portraits that had nothing at all macabre about them; the hands joined in prayer and the facial expression became the essential elements of the personality, as can be seen from recumbent figures in Dijon (128) and Pamplona (129). Portraits of women became more frequent (130, 131, 132), and children's portraits appeared in the sixteenth century: the princely recumbent figures of the children of Charles VIII in the cathedral of Tours; Charles Orlendo praying in the Louvre, by the master of Moulins; a little Montmorency at Taverny. The quest for resemblance can be regarded as a definite stage in the process of individualization that took place in the later Middle Ages. It stimulated two divergent trends in tombs during the sixteenth and seventeenth centuries: one toward intimacy, the other toward the triumphal.

These portraits represented the entire body. Beginning in the sixteenth century, the tomb with praying figure became simpler (exceptions were the great kneeling statues that were limited to personages of the highest status, anxious to display themselves as such).

Others, much more numerous, had less ambitious intentions but still desired their tombs to uphold their reputations and perpetuate their memory. Mural ornamentation became much more discreet, the better to concentrate attention upon two identificatory elements, the inscription and the portrait. But the latter now shrank to the dimensions of a bust, which either incorporated the gesture of the hands joined in prayer (133) or consisted of no more than the head (134). The value accorded to resemblance and all that it could reveal of the personality led to the retention of only the most individualized part of the body, the part that made recognition possible—namely, the face.

When the praying figure shifted from the tomb or altarpiece to the home and study, stripped of the religious scene and reduced to a

135

135. Tomb of the widow Olympia
Mangonia. Church of Santa Maria del
Popolo, Rome.

136. Façade of a tomb in the church
of Santa Maria Zobenigo o del Giglio
(1680–1683), Venice.

painted portrait (135), it often depicted the face alone, either from the front or in profile (as on Hellenistic and Roman coins, which may have inspired the choice of such a position).

In the seventeenth and eighteenth centuries, the similarities between the church mural-tomb and the secularized portrait became accentuated: the stone bust was in some cases replaced by a painting in which coloring enhanced the realism. Later, in the eighteenth century, it was a veritable salon painting that angels or allegorical virtues would bear aloft to heaven as a symbol of the soul.

This reduction to a domestic portrait was one of the new tendencies of funerary iconography in the modern period. The other tendency led to the public monument, the standing statue—in the case, clearly, of illustrious men.

It is as if the great kneeling, praying figures had stood up. One can see this in Venice (136), and it was not limited to doges. The Barbaros had their own church, which was both a family tomb and the seat of their devotions, just like the Bolognettis' church of Gesù e Maria in Rome.

In illustration 136 the principal family members —at the top the great admiral in his uniform, and below, nearer the level of the street and passers-by, the other members of the family in their wigs and robes— are displayed on the church's façade. It is true that in Venice church façades had served as secular memorials for two centuries, and imposing architectural tombs featuring standing commanders had long been customary; but the significance of these great statues is that they seem about to descend from their pedestals to the street or the square. In many English tombs of the eighteenth century the standing effigy also began to anticipate the public stance. And indeed it was in England that statues of politicians, philanthropists, and royalty first proliferated in the streets and squares at the beginning of the nineteenth century.

The tomb becomes bourgeois

It would probably not have been possible to penetrate the meaning of such a coherent and long-lasting iconography without methodically tracing the homogeneous series of recumbent and praying figures through several centuries. Nevertheless, it would be mistaken to believe that all the tombs of that long period belonged to the same formal type. We will leave royal and pontifical monuments out of our considerations, since they show too much of the creativity of great art to express any common denominator of culture at a more general level.

Most ordinary tombs resisted the prestige of imagery longer than might be expected, remaining tenaciously faithful to archaic formulas of the epitaph—formulas in which it had made its timid reappearance after centuries of anonymity, with the aim of making known the identity of the deceased.

We must suppose that in the churches of the thirteenth century such inscriptions filled the gaps left by the effigy-bearing tombs; they must have covered the walls, floors, and pillars. The starkness of the epigraphy no doubt reflected a spontaneous resistance to the icon and to a precise rendering of its eschatological content.

But beginning in the fourteenth century, resistance of that kind seems to have weakened—temporarily, at least. Here and there, epigraphy began to be affected by the contagion of imagery, but imagery of a very discreet kind which did no more than illustrate a text, without in any way distorting the sense. An example is the delicate recumbent figure in the center of a 1370 epitaph (137), an inscription of archaic

brevity. More frequently, such an illustration would adopt the theme of the praying figure in conjunction with a religious scene.

The tombs in illustrations 138 and 139, which both represent the same sacred object — the veil of Saint Veronica, bearing the imprint of the face of Christ — illustrate the progress made by the inscription. The loquacious fifteenth-century inscription mentions the families of the deceased and explains how both died at the same time in the course of "a great death" (the plague). These epitaphs also show how the size and originality of the image diminished, to the profit of the text. The sixteenth-century epitaph of Jean le Cauchoix and his wife (who are represented as praying figures at the top) is first and foremost a funerary panegyric (or elegy), followed by a classical poem on the subject of death composed by their son and heir, Jean, who also designed the monument (140).

These tombs are revealing examples of a model that is extremely common until the beginning of the eighteenth century. It conveyed two almost contradictory sentiments: first, a desire to represent the deceased in heaven with at least an illusion of resemblance; second, the eventual preference for text over image as an adequate means of summing up the merits of the deceased and expressing the filial or conjugal piety of the survivors. It is a curious fact that originally, in an oral culture and by means of very concise forms, the epitaph had served as an affirmation of identity, and that later, at the beginning of the modern period, and despite the encroachments of the effigy and the image, it rediscovered the Latin power of expression and all its rhetorical tradition, displacing an iconography that had become overly theatrical.

A new element also favored this development — an element that can be detected in two Marville tombs of the seventeenth century, one a mural (143), the other a horizontal tombstone (141). A brief line appears at

137. Epitaph dating from 1370. Musée des Augustins, Toulouse.

138. Funerary relief with veil of
Saint Veronica, by Philippe Piter
(fourteenth century). Musée des
Augustins, Toulouse.

139. Funerary relief with veil of
Saint Veronica. Church of
Saint-Eucaire, Metz.

the end of each inscription: in the first case, "having left to the brotherhood of Saint-Rosaire the sum of one thousand francs," and, in the second, "who [the deceased] endowed two anniversary services for this chapel, one on 13 September and the other on 8 November, in perpetuity" *(à toujours [et à ja]mais).* Could it be that the purpose of the tomb was no longer to perpetuate the likeness or merits of the deceased, or to symbolize his ascent to heaven, or even to solicit prayers from the passer-by on his behalf—that it now had another aim, perfectly defined by the two epitaphs? Hardly any importance was now attached to the ordinary little image at the top of the mural stela, which only barely recalled the praying figure—and which was eventually to be replaced on English headstones by a winged head. The epitaph was no longer a biographical announcement proclaiming the merits and piety of the deceased. It had become a reputedly imperishable monument ensuring the publicity—and consequently the durability—of a bargain struck between earthly possessors and representatives of the beyond. The exchanges (wealth in return for religious services) provided for in the deceased's testament were the object of a notarized contract, and the epitaph on the tomb gives the name of the notary and a detailed description of the legacies and donations, the services obtained in exchange from the church, and the conditions that would ensure the perpetuation of the arrangement.

The text of the epitaph corresponds to that of a last will and testament, which, from at least the sixteenth century to the early eighteenth, became an essential means by which a man set his affairs in order at his death (142, 144). It is worth noting that the name of the notary figures on the tomb as prominently as those of the deceased and his heir. He is, indeed, just as essential a personage. His chambers are the place where, in the course of a procedure both civil and mystical, communications are set up between heaven and earth.

It sometimes happened that such epitaphs for the departed soul were added to an effigy-bearing tomb, as we have seen. More often, though, they themselves served as tombs. A brief "here lies" *(cy-gist)* of three lines (lacking in illustrations 142 and 144) would sometimes precede the long and detailed description of the gifts and endowments and of the religious services obtained in exchange for them.

On the evidence of this type of document, at the end of the seventeenth century, one gets the impression that the dualistic concept of the human being—body versus soul—had been perfectly assimilated; that the body had been abandoned to its fate, underground or in a charnel house, while the soul, the immortal receptacle of the personality, concentrated upon itself all the capacities of the being as a whole. It had become—at the expense of the body—the sole object of the solicitude of the Church and the piety of the individual. This could not happen without a certain asceticism, leading to a scorn for the body; and this development might well have been a means through which death, held in abeyance for the time being, once again came to the fore.

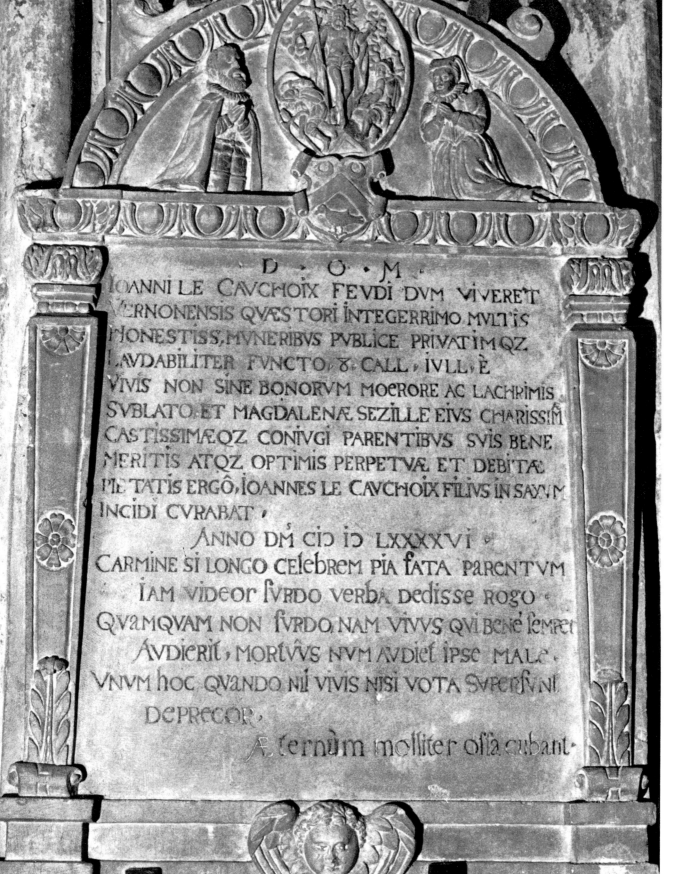

· D · O · M ·
IOANNI LE CAVCHOIX FEVDI DVM VIVERET
VERNONENSIS QVÆSTORI INTEGERRIMO MVLTIS
HONESTISS, MVNERIBVS PVBLICE PRIVATIMQZ
LAVDABILITER FVNCTO· 8· CALL· IVLL· È
VIVIS NON SINE BONORVM MOERORE AC LACHRIMIS
SVBLATO· ET MAGDALENÆ SEZILLE EIVS CHARISSIM
CASTISSIMÆQZ CONIVGI PARENTIBVS SVIS BENE
MERITIS ATQZ OPTIMIS PERPETVÆ ET DEBITÆ
PIETATIS ERGÔ, IOANNES LE CAVCHOIX FILIVS IN SAXVM
INCIDI CVRABAT·
        ANNO DM CIƆ IƆ LXXXXVI·
CARMINE SI LONGO CELEBREM PIA FATA PARENTVM
      IAM VIDEOR SVRDO VERBA DEDISSE ROGO·
QVAMQVAM NON SVRDO, NAM VIVVS QVI BENE SEMPER
      AVDIERIT, MORTVVS NVM AVDIET IPSE MALE·
VNVM HOC QVANDO NIL VIVIS NISI VOTA SVPERSVNT
      DEPRECOR·
              Æternùm molliter ossa cubant·

141 and 143. Epitaphs in the church of Saint-Nicolas, Marville, Meuse.

142 and 144. Donation plaques (seventeenth century). Arthies, Yvelines.

145. Reliquary of San Millán (1053–1067). Church of San Millán de la Cogolla, Old Castille.

146. Jan Polak, *The Dormition of the Virgin* (fifteenth or sixteenth century). Musée de Metz.

3. From the home to the grave

The deathbed   In this chapter we shall follow the series of images that describe the path traversed between death at home and burial of the body, taking in the laying out of the corpse, the funeral procession, and the church service—which are like so many climaxes punctuating the route and whose symbolic meanings have changed over the centuries as emphasis has moved from one to another, like a tonic accent, in a fashion that is faithfully conveyed by the relevant imagery.

Collected here is a sample of images that range from the Middle Ages to the present day and that depict "the recumbent figure sick in bed" referred to in ancient wills, or the "deathbed scene," as American anthropologists call it.

First, let us cast a rapid glance over the entire series. Despite the stylistic differences that reflect the originality of each period, it is impossible not to be struck by a family resemblance: the setting is always the same, the center of the scene is always the sick person in bed, and the room is always crowded with people. Even when the crowd is reduced to family members, the latter always appear numerous and crowded together. The deathbed abhors a vacuum; the action is a public one. This is the first thing that strikes us.

Now let us look at the situation more closely. A number of distinctions can be made within our collection. Two quite separate groups appear, one depicting a Christian death, the other a lay or secularized one. These are customarily set in opposition—let's admit it.

Consider first the presentiment of death. In the past, death did not strike without warning. At San Millán de la Cogolla (eleventh century), a man lies on his bed, wrapped in a thick coverlet, with one hand raised (145); at the bedside, an angel reveals to him that he is about to die *(transitus).*

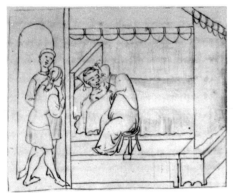

147 and 148. Illustrations from Boccaccio's *Decameron* (fourteenth century). Bibliothèque Nationale, Paris.

Toward the other end of the Middle Ages, a Bocaccio illustration entrusts the angel's role to death, who hovers in the air while an epidemic of plague rages; the figure of death points at the sick man it is about to carry off (147).

The man knows that his end is near: some kind of social ceremony is beginning in the room, around the bed. It is a ceremony that was often depicted at the end of the Middle Ages and thereafter, but it is harder to imagine it in earlier periods because then the iconography represented it only in the case of saints. We must accept that fact and recognize that there was a close relationship between those exemplary and exceptional deaths of saints and the deaths of more ordinary men even if, in moving from the former to the latter, the intensity, solemnity, and number of rites were diminished—indeed, debased.

From the middle of the medieval period to the seventeenth century, the death that was most often depicted was that of the Virgin. The name used to refer to it—the *dormitio* (sleep)—was borrowed from the ancient funerary terminology of the early Church. For centuries it remained the prototype of the good death, until in the seventeenth century the less miraculous—and also more intimate, not to say solitary—death of Saint Joseph became more popular.

The dormition of Metz (146) or that of Triel (I), just two of innumerable examples, will allow us to reconstruct the ceremony. The Virgin lies in a monumental bed. The apostles crowd round her, playing the role that normally falls to the clergy. One of them is placing in the hand of the dying Virgin a candle that she no longer has the strength to hold. The others are celebrating the ceremony of the absolution: the celebrant, Saint Peter, recognizable by his archbishop's pallium, is sprinkling the body of the Virgin with a holy-water sprinkler which he dips into a bowl held by an acolyte. A second apostle-priest is blowing on the coals of his incense burner. Another is reading liturgical prayers from a book held open before him.

This is the rite which today is called the absolution and which in the sixteenth and seventeenth centuries was known by the first word of its anthem, the *libera*. It was—and still is today—recited over the coffin in church or over the tomb in the cemetery. Here it is pronounced over the deathbed itself, just before death. The practice of performing absolution in the bedchamber at the deathbed itself later disappeared, probably replaced by the private confession, as seen in Boccaccio (148).

In the Pamplona tympanum (149), where the Virgin, already dead, is about to be wrapped—and with such care!—in her winding sheet, the crowding of the space is increased by the procession of angels accompanying Christ, who has come to fetch his mother's soul.

Such scenes of absolution were not limited to the dormition of the Virgin: they were identical for saints. The body was always laid out on a bed; however, in earlier periods this was not the monumental marriage bed of the fifteenth and sixteenth centuries but a portable one, of the type used by travelers when they stopped for the night. In the case of monks and prelates, who were assimilated to saints, the dying man would be carried to church, where he would receive the last sacrament and the final unction, die, and be laid out and "absolved." The scene was considered so important that it was sometimes reproduced on tombs—as, for example, on a mural tomb in Perpignan (150). We recognize here the protagonists of the familiar liturgy: the cross bearer and two candle bearers surround the celebrant, together with two other

I. Jean le Prince, *The Dormition of the Virgin* (sixteenth century). Church of Triel-sur-Seine, Yvelines.

II. Illumination from *Treatise and Commentary on Medicine,* by Galen and others (early fourteenth century). Bibliothèque Municipale, Rheims. (See p. 110).

III. *Burial* (fifteenth century). Bibliothèque Municipale, Lyons. (See p. 131.)

IV. Hans Baldung Grien, *Portrait of a Lady* (1530). Thyssen-Bornemisza Collection, Lugano, Switzerland. (See p. 202.)

V. Trophime Bigot, *Saint Sebastian Tended by Saint Irene* (seventeenth century), detail. Musée des Beaux-Arts, Bordeaux. (See p. 210.)

VI. J. H. Fuseli, *Brunhild and Gunther* (eighteenth century). Nottingham Museum, England. (See p. 211.)

VII. Painted brooch depicting
Louisa Hairston at her mother's tomb
(1805), by Thomas Sully. Collection
of Douglas H. Gordon. (See p. 247.)

VIII. Jarvis Hanks, *Death Scene*
(1840–1842). Campus Martius
Museum, Marietta, Ohio.
(See p. 247.)

IX. George Cochran Lambdin, *The Dead Wife* (late nineteenth century). North Carolina Museum of Art, Raleigh, gift of P. A. Vogt. (See p. 254.)

149

149. Dormition of the Virgin.
Cathedral of Pamplona, Navarre.

150. Funerary slab (thirteenth
century). Cathedral of Perpignan.

150

clerics, one holding the sprinkler and the bowl of holy water, the other the incense burner.

The death of Saint Francis was also modeled on the traditional death of the Virgin. In illustration 151, a painting dating from the fourteenth or fifteenth century, he is seen laid out in church upon a stretcher whose canvas is attached to the wooden sides by ropes. The scene represents the moment at which the celebrant censes the body. The crowd of monks and laymen presses in closely all around.

Frequently, a single bas-relief shows the two scenes, or rather the two absolutions, in sequence: first the deathbed, then the entombment. These were the two climactic moments of the funeral rite throughout the first half of the Middle Ages—and sometimes a little later.

A fourteenth-century tomb in Burgos (152a) includes an extra detail that is a common feature in Spanish art: the gesticulations of the mourners (152b). In Mediterranean countries, agitated manifestations of grief usually took place in the bedroom, around the deathbed. Elsewhere, mourning was calmer, or was made calmer, ritualized; and it was, out of preference, reserved for the funeral procession.

Examples of Christian death scenes of nonsaints are rarer and of later date. At first they were modeled upon the deaths of saints, to whom great laymen and clergy were thus assimilated: the sarcophagus of Raymond Béranger, preserved at Ripoll (153), was designed on the same model and depicts the same series of climactic points.

From the fifteenth century on, the theme became more common. It appeared illustrated in books of devotions, which were designed initially for the use of an elite of literate laymen but which, later, with the advent of printing, reached a wider clientele. These were the books of hours (of which we have already noticed a number in the hands of certain female recumbent figures).

In an engraving of 1547, the death of an old woman is used to illustrate both the last phase of life and also the way that it corresponds to the last month of the calendar year (154). The arrangement of the

151. Iacopo Avanzi, *The Funeral Rites of Saint Francis* (fourteenth or fifteenth century). Vatican Pinacoteca, Rome.

152a and 152b. Tomb of bishop Gonzola de Hinojosa (died 1320), detail and overall view. San Gregorio chapel, cathedral of Burgos.

153. Tomb of Raymond Bérenger III (died 1131). Monastery of Santa Maria, Ripoll, Catalonia.

154. Engraving from the *Heures à l'usage de Toul* (1547). Musée Lorrain, Nancy.

155. *The Last Rites* (fifteenth century). Musée Bonnat, Bayonne.

figures is still reminiscent of the scenes of the Virgin's death or those of the saints. A priest steadies a candle in the hand of the dying woman, as in the Metz dormition scene. Men and women crowd solicitously around the bed, but the rites of absolution have disappeared.

These rites were replaced either by the private confession (148) or by the last Communion, which was always an important and solemn ceremony in the ancient liturgy and which now became the major ceremony of death. A fifteenth-century painting (155) gives a good idea of it; the painting may have adorned the chapel of some brotherhood, as an illustration of the members' good works. A Dominican monk is giving Communion to a sick, bedridden man, assisted by the wife and a servant. He has come to the house from the monastery church, at the head of a procession of at least twelve men (the number of the Apostles?). One carries a lantern, the others candles.

The scene was already an established one at the time, and was to be repeated virtually unchanged until the beginning of the twentieth century. It presented one of the most common images of death. Neighbors, friends, relatives, and passers-by would follow the priest (perhaps encountered quite by chance in the street), who carried the Corpus Christi and was preceded by a little acolyte with his lantern and bell. They would accompany him to the bedroom, which at that point ceased to be a private space and became a place of meeting and public prayer, as the painting by François Brillaud shows (156).

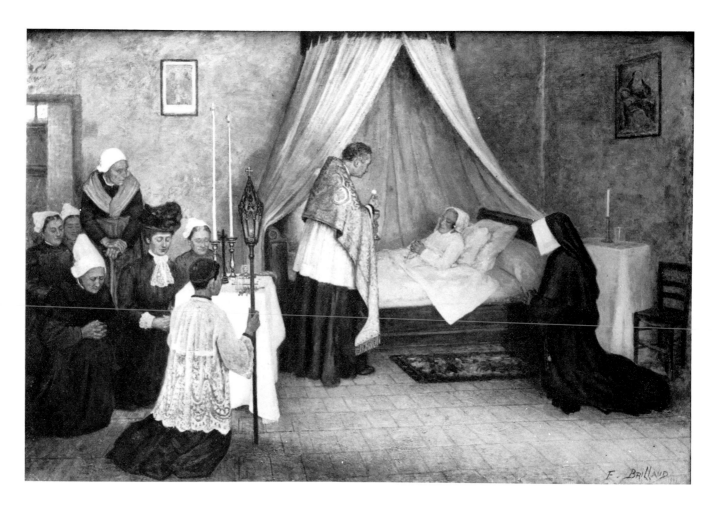

156. François Brillaud, *Last Rites in the Vendée* (1910).

We now come to the second group of images in our sample of deathbed scenes. What is striking here is that the religious references have disappeared.

In the first place, altogether new models appeared, borrowed from pagan antiquity; their popularity in the eighteenth century suggests that they responded to some kind of need. They represent the death of a sage — of Socrates (157), Cato (158), or Seneca: a willed death, a suicide but not in secret, rather one that appropriated at least the publicity of the traditional kind of death.

The *philosophes* of the eighteenth century and the "secular" moralists and atheists of the nineteenth were to identify with such scenes and oppose them to the Christian models, which had in the meantime become increasingly aggressive, being presented as de facto arguments against the free-thinkers.

Although this new image of death certainly manifests a rejection of a "Catholicism obsessed with death" (the phrase, *catholicisme morticole*, is that of R. Favre), we must be on our guard: it does not deny the moral importance of death, does not present death as merely a transition to nothingness. Julie's death in *La Nouvelle Héloïse* corresponds, in its own simpler and more natural way, to the great examples of the "saints" of antiquity: there is still a relationship between the dignity of life and that of death. In a note cited by R. Favre (p. 168), J.-J. Rousseau comments: "Death, even more than life, should express the *deeper being* [my italics], rather than present an occasion for a new role" (that of Christian eschatology). For Julie, death is the moment of plentitude, of a consciousness of life: "Oh death, come when you will." And, according to G. Chaussinand-Nogaret's description, that is just how it was for Mirabeau too: "He died very simply, not with the resignation of a Christian but with the resolve of a sage of antiquity, like a Stoic, surrounded by his friends, talking with them of things of this world, undisturbed by a beyond in which he did not believe . . . In the early hours of the following morning, on 2 April, he prepared himself for death. 'My friend,' he said to Cabanis, 'today I shall die. When one reaches this point, only one thing remains to be done: to perfume oneself, crown oneself with flowers [the influence of Antiquity], and surround oneself with music so as to attain in an agreeable fashion that *sleep* [my italics] from which there is no awakening.' Then he lost the power of speech."

With Greuze (159), the genre painting returned to the theme. Two new psychological elements were now combined with dignity and publicity, the previously essential characteristics. The first was pathos. Neither medieval death scenes nor the death of David's Socrates is truly pathetic. Death as portrayed in the works of Greuze or in Guerin's painting of Cato (158) is.

But death as depicted by Caravaggio already was pathetic: his paintings, to my mind, represent a link between the two images, the Christian and the secular. Is there anything specifically Christian about his *Death of the Virgin* (161)? It shows simply the death of an ordinary woman, in a room full of people.

Christian painters of the nineteenth century were, doubtless unconsciously, following the models of an iconography no longer Christian. Consider Jacquand's painting of 1875 (160). Remove the priest figure of Saint Peter, added as a startling extra to the scene, and what you have left is a composition in the style of Greuze (note in passing, on the right, the presence of a small boy; in 1875, that had no shock impact).

The priest has disappeared: this is the essential fact. One or two—not unambiguous—details remained: a crucifix above the bed, the children's clasped hands (162); but the solemn rites of a Christian death, deemed superstitious, were now avoided.

The other psychological element, which appeared at about the same time as pathos and combined with it, eventually altered the whole significance of the deathbed scene. It perhaps truly marked the beginning of the privatization of death, a process that has continued until the present day. The new element was intimacy. It appeared at the end of the eighteenth century—indeed, as early as the mid-seventeenth in Puritan England. Thus, the corpse of a relative of Samuel Pepys, because it smelled so strongly, was banished to the courtyard (albeit accompanied by two servants with more resistance to the smell). The gathering in the bedroom became more restricted. Presence at the deathbed now seemed to be reserved for the closest and most grief-stricken relatives, children included (163).

The dying person was not left alone, though; there were still people present in the room, even if it was no longer accessible to all and sundry. The real or imaginary dialogue between the dying or deceased person and a few relatives persisted.

However, this initial tendency toward privacy seems to have been interrupted in the second half of the nineteenth century. The dying person's room, which had briefly become emptier, filled up again, as can be seen in a German painting of the early twentieth century (164) —the period of Munch, who was so obsessed with death. Agitated

157. Jacques Louis David, *The Death of Socrates* (1787). Metropolitan Museum of Art, New York.

158. Pierre Narcisse Guérin, *The Death of Cato of Utica* (1797). École des Beaux-Arts, Paris.

159. Jean-Baptiste Greuze, *The Punished Son* (1778). Musée du Louvre, Paris.

women crowd around the dying figure. Is it just by chance that they are all women, as is also the case in the nearly contemporary painting shown in illustration 156? Was death tending to become an affair for women?

There is one more testimony to the return (if that is what it really was) of the complete family gathering at the deathbed—preferably a large family quite willing to include sons and daughters-in-law to swell the numbers. Consider the Italian funerary sculpture of the late nineteenth century. Men are present as well as women; here the latter have no monopoly over mourning. The entire, attentive family is either watching for the dying breath of the beloved relative or seeking to prolong his presence by remaining at his side, as if refusing to accept separation (165).

The moment remains an important and solemn one, but the mixture of pathos and family intimacy turns it into a time of separation and inconsolable grief.

There is a fundamental difference between the intimate death shown at the end of the eighteenth century and the death in solitude.

The fact is that for a long time common opinion identified poverty with solitude. The poor man was primarily a man alone (Michel Mollat). He ran the risk of remaining alone, even in death.

In the Middle Ages, the most hated death was considered that of the traveler abandoned by the roadside or in the water. The secularization of the nineteenth century in no way changed this abhorrence of isolation at the moment when it was the hardest to bear: in a scene showing a

158

159

162. Engraving of a deathbed scene (late eighteenth century). Musée Carnavalet, Paris.

163. Achille Devéria, *Day of Grief* (c. 1835). Musée Carnavalet, Paris.

164. A. Jank, *Around a Dying Man* (Germany, c. 1900). Bibliothèque des Arts Décoratifs, Paris.

165. Funerary sculpture. Staglieno Cemetery, Genoa.

164

165

166. Léonie Humbert-Vignot, *Poor Folk* (1908).

traditional solidarity offered by the community and the family, and to shut himself or herself away in solitude. Note that there is not a single sign of hope, Christian or otherwise, in illustration 168. In pious circles in the seventeenth century, the solitude of the tête-à-tête with the priest was extended to include the period preceding the death throes: the dying person, having, as was customary, bid farewell to his sometimes large entourage, would ask to be left alone with God.

At the end of the Middle Ages, there were two other instances in which an unaccustomed solitude prevailed: the private confession (148) and the — still infrequent — medical consultation (II), two spatial intervals newly won from the promiscuities of collective life and reserved for the dying person's tête-à-tête with the priest or the medical practitioner.

First poverty and then (more surreptitiously) self-love and the practices of confession and medical consultation: these were the three factors that were beginning to separate the dying person from his community and turn him in toward himself.

The Christian and philosophical concepts of death both shun the extreme of solitude.

Furthermore, they both express a common desire for solidarity and

Plate II: following page 96.

110

publicity and ascribe equal measures — if different types — of dignity to the final moment.

In the mid-twentieth century, however, a new model arose within the intellectual elites of the Western societies that exert so much influence on human ways of thinking.

It is a model that is difficult to illustrate using images — in contrast to the earlier types, which present an overabundance of choices. The only image which might be suitable is that of the hospital's replacing the home. But thanks to new medical techniques, the seriously ill who lie in hospitals retain, in principle, every chance of recovery; and in the most desperate cases, everything possible is arranged so as to prevent their identifying themselves with the dying.

So, this once, we shall do without an image and instead employ the abstraction of the written word. Below are reproduced, as epigraphic texts, two comments, one by an American historian, Paul Robinson, the other by a French philosopher, Bernard Rousset:

Perhaps more fundamentally I disagree with Ariès's proposition that death is one of the great existential truths whose reality we must constantly reaffirm. The neglect of death — its reduction "to the insignificance of an ordinary event" — is, I would argue, a measure of our psychic maturity . . . Death may have been such in the past [a great central fact of life], but I see nothing lost — and much gained — in its relegation to the periphery of human experience.

— Paul Robinson, "Five Models for Dying," 1981

167. Lithograph by Nanteuil, after A. Etex, *The Death of the Proletarian* (1844). Bibliothèque Nationale, Paris.

LA DÉLIVRANCE
OU LA MORT DU PROLÉTAIRE

There is a huge temptation — and it is a great danger — to mask the truth about death and the dead, nothingness. Traditional societies have seen death as implying and conferring a meaning, and one of a superior kind. Most metaphysical systems have followed them and the social sciences often do likewise, laying emphasis upon the negative aspect of our modern civilization, which is incapable of accommodating death and the dead. But a truly philosophical lucidity should not follow their example. [It should recognize] that death and the dead are nothing and hold no significance at all.
— Bernard Rousset, "La Philosophie devant la mort," 1975

These two inscriptions provide a good definition of the most radical view of death today (possibly a minority attitude but one that is gaining ground). We should consider them, and compare them with all that has previously been said about the deathbed. There is a glaring difference: it is apparent that the Christian death and the death of the sage, despite the opposition between them, belong to the same civilization and the same existential background. The great cultural rift does not pass between them but between, on the one hand, the vast domain of death in a major key, be it Christian or secular, and, on the other, death in a minor key, which is the death of today, foreshadowed by unobtrusive signs as early as the late eighteenth century.

Exhibiting the corpse and laying it in the coffin

In the nineteenth century and occasionally even today, the deceased is displayed on the deathbed in the attitude of a medieval recumbent figure, nowadays dressed in his or her best nightshirt or Sunday clothes or wedding costume (169).

This is not a very old custom, dating back in all likelihood hardly beyond the nineteenth century. In Merovingian burial grounds of the Frankish period, the bodies of both women and men were probably clothed, but in the Middle Ages that practice disappeared or was preserved only in the case of prelates, clergymen, kings, and knights, all of whom would be dressed in the distinctive costume of their respective functions (Madame de Sévigné was buried at Grignan "dressed in blue brocade"). In the case of priests, the custom persisted.

All other bodies were left in their shifts or simply unclothed — but not for long, since they would soon be moved out of the bedroom.

The nineteenth-century practice of laying out the corpse on the bed and dressing it up probably corresponded to a new interval between the moment of death and the arrival of visitors. When the bedroom was reserved until the moment of death for the family alone, the visitors would come *afterward* — "viewing the remains," as the custom was called in would-be innovative America (previously, visitors had come before or during the death).

In those days, the body was exhibited in the bedroom, on the deathbed. Previously (from the sixteenth to the eighteenth century), it had also been exhibited, but only very briefly and not in the house itself (except where the aristocracy was concerned) but at the door, out in the street. There, the corpse would be laid out on straw — probably a monastic ritual expressing a quest for humility, and still practiced in Holland in Calvinist times. From the fifteenth and sixteenth centuries on, what must have started as a simple layer of rushes was replaced by a mat of straw with one end rolled up like a bolster to support the head. An example can be seen in illustration 170, depicting a plague epidemic. It is also suggested in de Witt's painting of the tomb of William

168. Illumination from the *Heures à l'usage de Paris,* known as *The Rohan Hours* (c. 1418). Bibliothèque Nationale, Paris.

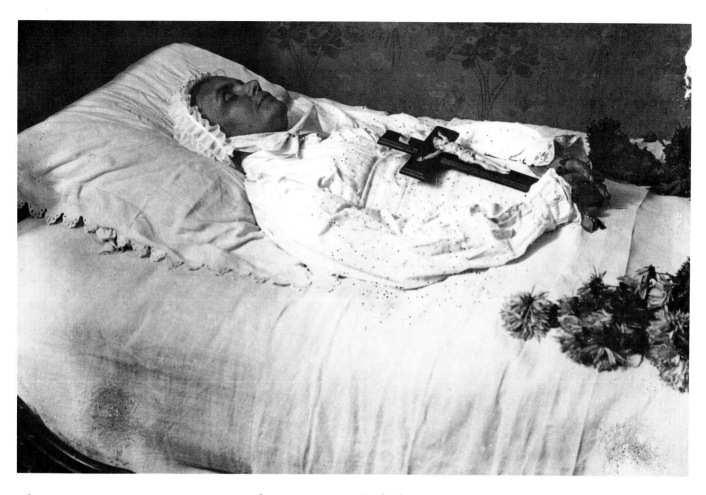

169. Deathbed, 1900.

of Orange in Delft (92). In the nineteenth century the practice of displaying the corpse in the coffin persisted in some areas, even if straw was not used. Illustration 171 shows this in the case of the funeral of a Breton sailor. Eventually the practice was replaced by the posting of a death notice in the same spot, at the transition point between house and street.

In the most ancient medieval representations, the body was exhibited even before death. The corpse would then be carried on a stretcher to the sarcophagus and there deposited, wrapped in a sheet (or winding sheet). Beginning in the middle of the medieval period, when wooden coffins were more generally used (either an individual, permanent coffin or a temporary, collective one used only for transporting the corpse), the body would be immediately wrapped in a sheet, called a shroud (*sudarium*) or winding sheet, and, in the case of the wealthy, placed in a coffin. Such is the scene depicted in a miniature from the *Heures de Neville* (172). The bowl of holy water and the sprinkler are placed on the floor; formerly they would have been at the bedside. This benediction, it seems to me, was probably a survival of the old absolution, now abandoned. Nearby, a woman is distributing bread to the poor; others present are given clothes. In England, in the seventeenth century and even later, ribbons, gloves, and rings would be distributed.

But, until the end of the eighteenth century, not everyone had the right to an individual coffin—far from it.

A miniature from the *Heures de Rohan* shows different categories of corpses lying in a cemetery strewn with bones (173). One body is laid out, naked, on a rich cloth. It will be carried away and deposited in a sarcophagus of stone or, as was more and more frequently the case, in a coffin of wood or lead. This is a person of importance. The other two are sewn into their shrouds, from head to foot (you can see the stitches). They will in all likelihood be buried like this, going straight into the ground, into the paupers' grave, without any coffin. In the seventeenth century these cheap shrouds were known as *serpillières* (*serpillière* was a type of coarse cloth, or sacking).

In the hospital of Bruges in the eighteenth century, corpses were simply wrapped in the straw on which they had been displayed, according to monastic custom (174).

Regarding this topic, we should note a difference between the north and the south in the manner of displaying the corpse. In northern cultures, the corpse was entirely covered and sewn in from head to foot, as can be seen in numerous illustrations from the thirteenth century (175) to the seventeenth (177—an illustration for the proverbs of Lagniet). In southern societies, in contrast, the old practice of the early Middle Ages continued to be followed, and the body, or at least the head, was left visible. It was a practice that survived nearly to the present day; the coffin was not closed until it reached the cemetery, and the winding sheet was left open to reveal the face (176). In Bologna, in a fresco in the church of San Petronio, there is even a strange coffin that anticipates the caskets seen in California today: it is being used for transporting the saint, and the lid has been cut so as to leave the face visible (178).

170. *The Plague* (late sixteenth century). Musée d'Histoire de la Médecine, Paris.

171

The funeral procession　At the beginning of the medieval period, the transportation of the body from the home to the monastery where it was to be buried (or to a large cemetery which might be shared by an entire valley) must have been such a simple affair that no illustrations were made of it. We know only what it was like to transport the relics of saints—on the shoulders of men, as in the case of Saint Stephen (179), or, when the distances were greater, by horse or mule (180). In these two examples, the coffin is preceded by a priest carrying a cross. The hand-carried coffin remained in use for a very long time in both town and countryside, where it was very popular until contemporary commercialization of funerals by private and municipal concerns replaced it with the horse-drawn hearse. Toward the end of the nineteenth century, the English imagined that in Paris the little coffins of poor children were still carried this way (181). Perhaps they were.

But beginning in the middle of the medieval period the transportation of the corpse to the burial ground lost that functional simplicity. It acquired and retained until the twentieth century (notwithstanding a few changes of fortune at the end of the eighteenth century) a special importance that it had not hitherto possessed. It turned into a solemn procession, initially religious and later secular.

Such ritualization implies some kind of protocol and also functionaries to apply it.

As to religious functionaries: First, chiefly in the towns, there were the "four mendicant orders," as they were called—the Dominicans (186), Franciscans, Carmelites, and Augustins. Then there were associations of pious laymen who regarded the burial of the dead as a work of charity comparable to visiting the sick or unfortunates in prison. These

116

171. Ulysse Butin, *A Sailor's Funeral* (1878).

172. Illumination from the *Heures de Neville* (c. 1435). Bibliothèque Nationale, Paris.

173. Illumination from the *Heures à l'usage de Paris,* known as *The Rohan Hours* (c. 1418). Bibliothèque Nationale, Paris.

172

173

174. Anonymous painting (eighteenth century). Musée Memling, Hôpital Saint-Jean, Bruges.

175. The resurrection of Lazarus, as depicted on a cathedral capital (thirteenth century). Tudela, Navarre.

176. Illumination showing Naomi grieving for her husband and sons, from the *Miroir de l'humaine salvation* (fifteenth century). Musée Condé, Chantilly.

177. Engraving by Lagniet (seventeenth century). Musée d'Histoire de la Médecine, Paris.

178. *Episodes in the Life of Saint Petronio* (detail). Fresco in the Bolognini chapel, basilica of San Petronio, Emilia-Romagna.

174

175

Noemy plangit maritu sui & filios

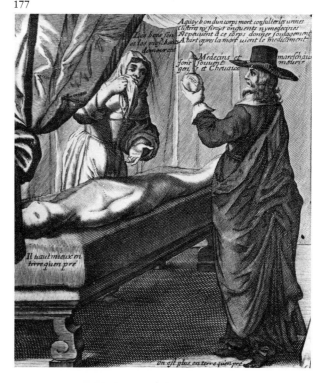

179. Transfer of the relics of Saint Stephen. Chevet capital, former priory of Lubersac, Corrèze.

associations were called brotherhoods, charities, or fraternities. Within the parish the brethren would play the role later assumed by undertakers, and also took it upon themselves to bury the poor. They would meet in their own chapel, where they kept the necessary materials — in particular the poles and lanterns that they would carry to burials and other ceremonies. In one of these chapels, in the church of Vétheuil, the ornamentation and some of the furnishings have been preserved. The chapel is very interesting. A large eighteenth-century painting shows the brethren performing their tasks (182). The same chapel also contains traces of an older painting from the sixteenth century, now almost effaced, which must have represented a similar burial scene but in which women too are present, recognizable from their headgear (183).

These brotherhoods remained in operation for a long time in country regions. In a painting by Ulysse Butin (171), the two men leading the procession are wearing over their shoulders scarves decorated with teardrops and crossed bones — the insignia of their brotherhood.

The brethren of Vétheuil are wearing short coats (182). More generally, functionaries wore a long robe with a hood, as did the more exotic southern brotherhoods of penitents. This was in fact the mourning cloak which would be distributed to all those taking part in a funeral. The funerary art of the fourteenth and fifteenth centuries, which gave special importance to the scene of the funeral procession, produced many representations of groups of mourners in their long robes (184). Two of the four figures carrying Abner's coffin in the *Heures de Condé* (185) might well be members of a brotherhood, to judge by their robes and hoods.

From this time on, there would be a long religious procession to take the body or coffin either to church or to the cemetery (186). Its solemnity would vary according to the rank that the deceased had held in the social hierarchy.

The crowning moment of the funeral ritual came no longer in the bedroom or the cemetery, or, necessarily, in the church, but in the funeral procession.

The church service　　Today, the church service is virtually the only funerary liturgical ceremony of the Roman Catholic Church. It is not the oldest, however. It was only toward the end of the Middle Ages and to an increasing degree later that a secular elite adopted the ancient clerical custom of taking the body to the church for a service at the altar, before proceeding to the burial ground.

Little by little, it became customary to have the body and the mourners enter the church to celebrate a high Mass for the repose of the soul. Such Masses were part of a system for staking a claim in the beyond — a system that had been in operation for a number of years and that included many other Masses, both high and low. The poor, who could not afford such services, had to be content with the attentions of a brotherhood, which would organize the funeral procession and the last absolution. So the poor would go directly to the cemetery without stopping at the church, just as everybody, apart from the clergy and great lords, had formerly done.

Now, the coffin deposited in the church before the altar where Mass was celebrated was more than just a presence: it almost immediately became the center of an impressive setting by which it was exalted and at the same time camouflaged. It was set on a raised platform, covered by a sheet or "pall," sometimes also by a kind of roof, and, above all, surrounded by torches and candles which illuminated it like a "chapel"—hence the name used to refer to it. Nowadays, the word "catafalque" is preferred. Beginning in the fourteenth century it became the center of a setting that was to assume positively extravagant proportions in the seventeenth and eighteenth centuries. Funeral ceremonies came to rival opera sets in ostentation, becoming another manifestation of Baroque theatricality. However, the differences in scale and dimensions are not really enough to break the continuity linking illustrations 187 and 188 (dating from the fifteenth century) with illustration 189 (dating from the early eighteenth), each of them chosen from among hundreds of others available. Personally, I am struck by the similarities among the various settings and the motivations behind them. That is why I consider the main cultural development in this domain, in the course of this long period, to be the creation in the church, during the second half of the medieval period, of a decorative space whose center was occupied by the concealed corpse.

Indeed, except where the face of the deceased was traditionally left uncovered, the corpse was either hidden inside the coffin or else obscured by the complicated décor.

But at about the same time there developed another custom, equally ostentatious, which aimed for a contrary effect — namely, to perpetuate the presence of the deceased by means of a portrait displayed in church during the funeral and subsequently (as we saw in Chapter 2) on the tomb. It was a curious historical sequence: there was now a new desire to affirm the personality of the deceased by displaying an image of his face. We must remember that, ever since the early Middle Ages, in church or monastic communities, the dying person had been carried to church on a stretcher or bier. There he would die, and remain while prayers for the dead were recited and a Mass was celebrated at the altar. We can see such scenes depicted in documents which date from

180. Tomb of Raymond Bérenger III (died 1131). Monastery of Santa Maria, Ripoll, Catalonia.

181. Reinhart, *A Child's Funeral in Paris* (1880). Bibliothèque des Arts Décoratifs, Paris.

121

e Gabriel **MORIN** Secretaire du Roi Bienfaiteur de cette Confrerie, decede a Paris en rsice, lui a Leguee par Testamment une somme de 300 qui ont ete employees en l'année 1773 pour L trefois aux depens de Robert Bouché prevot et de Jean Grisau echevin...Elle fut restaurée en 1829

182 and 183. Frescoes (eighteenth and sixteenth century, respectively). Vétheuil church, Yvelines.

184. Mourners at the tomb of Jean sans Peur (died 1419) and Marguerite de Bavière. Musée des Beaux-Arts, Dijon.

185. Illumination showing David mourning at Abner's funeral, from the *Miroir de l'humaine salvation* (fifteenth century). Musée Condé, Chantilly.

184

Overleaf:

186. Illumination from the *Histoire d'Olivier de Castille et Artus Algarbe* (fifteenth century). Bibliothèque Nationale, Paris.

187. Illumination from the *Heures à l'usage de Rome* (c. 1480). Bibliothèque Nationale, Paris.

188. Illumination from *Le Miroir historial* of Vincent de Beauvais (fifteenth century). Musée Condé, Chantilly.

189. Mourning scene in honor of a prince of Saxony (Germany, early eighteenth century). Musée Carnavalet, Paris.

185

186

a later period but which hark back to earlier times and record the old practices (190).

Around the thirteenth century, the corpse ceased to be considered fit for display, and was customarily concealed with a sewn-up shroud, a coffin, a catafalque. However, in funerals of monks and great lords, both secular and clerical, the older custom continued for a while. In the case of royalty, the development of the cult of the monarchy reinforced the tradition: the king does not die. He must therefore be preserved and put on display after his death — not as a dead man but, like a modern Californian, with every appearance of life. This practice was imitated by the aristocracy, leading to the development of embalming at the end of the Middle Ages.

The body would then be displayed as shown in illustrations 191 and 193.

Subsequently, members of royalty, too, developed an aversion to the sight of the corpse. This distaste affected every level of society, spreading upward until it reached even the most conservative aristocratic milieux.

Here, at this point, a new idea emerged — that of creating a double for the deceased. The corpse would be shut away after a short while and replaced, for a longer period of display, by what was called a "representation" — that is, an effigy in wood or wax.

The cenotaph now took the form of a coffin with an effigy lying on top of it, as in illustration 192. This practice was abandoned at the end of the sixteenth century in France, but it persisted in England, where some of these royal representations are preserved in Westminster Abbey.

187

188

189

HONORI · ET · MEMORIAE
SERENISSIMI · PRINCIPIS
CHRISTIANI · AVGVSTI
PR · ANH · DVCIS · SAX · ANG · ET · WESTPH · COMITIS
ASC · DNI · S · B · I · ET · K · SVPREMI · CASTRORVM · REGIAE
MAIEST · BORVSS · PRAEFECTI · STETINI · GVBERNATO
RIS · EQVITIS · ORDINIS · AQVILAE · NIGRAE · ET
TRIBVNI · LEGIONIS · PEDESTRIS
SACRAT · VIDVA · MAESTISSIMA

190

190. Miniature depicting obsequies for the abbess of the Sisters of Charity of Venice (sixteenth century).

191. Jean Perréal, *The Arrival of the Queen's Body and Its Reception by Cardinal Jean de Luxembourg* (1515). Musée du Petit-Palais, Paris.

191

192

192. Jean Perréal, *Service in the Church of the Savior, Blois* (1515). Musée du Petit-Palais, Paris.

193. Illumination depicting the funeral of Jeanne de Bourbon, from the *Grandes Chroniques de France* (c. 1375). Bibliothèque Nationale, Paris.

193

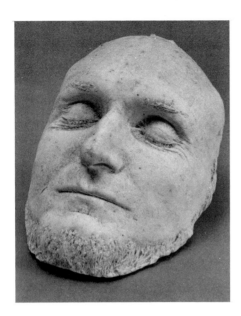

194. Death mask of Alexis Dupont (nineteenth century). Hagley Museum and Library, Wilmington, Delaware.

The representation made sense only if it was as true a likeness as possible. Such a resemblance would be obtained by making a plaster cast of the face of the deceased. In order to achieve a good likeness, the features of death were reproduced. Funerary masks thus became a means of capturing a true likeness and also — strangely enough — of creating an illusion of life. The sixteenth-century workshop that produced the terracotta statues for the ambulatory of the abbey of Saint-Sernin in Toulouse used death masks to make them look lifelike. They were known as "the counts' mummies" (195, 196) because they were believed to represent the counts of Toulouse who had been benefactors of the abbey in the Middle Ages.

It now became standard practice to make a death mask. Pascal's mask, for example, is well known. Curiously, as time passed, the macabre quality of the realism that is so striking in the Saint-Sernin statues was muted, giving way to an expression of serenity or even beauty. Death masks no longer simulated life but instead registered an ideal attitude which the nineteenth century considered to be the prerogative of death (194). It was no offense to good taste to hang death masks such as these on the walls of one's home.

The prolonged exhibition of the corpse, the choice of a favorite spot for its burial, and the practice of bringing the dead home from distant battlefields all encouraged the practice of embalming in the second half of the Middle Ages.

The internal organs, which were removed from the body, were often placed in a separate tomb. There were tombs for intestines, such as that of Charles V (197), and, even more frequently, tombs for the heart (198). The heart acquired a very strong symbolic significance, reaching a peak in the eighteenth century, the period of great devotion to the Sacred Heart. But that significance has since been lost; today the heart is an organ like any other. The symbolism explains why it was considered important to preserve the heart and why such care was taken to assign it a destination of its own which was different from that of the body. In England, as late as the early nineteenth century, members of the royal family were still embalmed and their entrails buried separately.

The inhumation Now we come to the last stage of the itinerary: the entombment, or inhumation. During the first half of the Middle Ages, until the funeral procession acquired the importance that we have seen, the entombment stood in a symmetrical relation to the deathbed. On tombs the two scenes are often depicted side by side (199) and, in every case, the same rite of absolution is represented: just as it was described above in the context of the death of the Virgin or the saints, we again find it taking place beside the sarcophagus in which the body has been deposited by *viri religiosi.* It has retained the same form right to the present day, with one essential difference — namely, that (apart from exceptional cases) today the absolution is no longer said at the place of burial but at the church. The clergy then retire, leaving the body to the undertakers and a handful of the closest relatives. History shows a gradual devaluation of entombment, though the process appears to have been irregular.

As we have observed, the process started when the particular importance formerly attached to the entombment shifted to the funeral procession and the church service. This evolution was hastened by the

195 and 196. "Mummies of the Counts" (c. 1500). Musée des Augustins, Toulouse.

197. Recumbent figure on the tomb of the entrails of Charles V (fourteenth century). Musée du Louvre, Paris.

198. Tomb plaque for the heart of Enguerrand VII, seigneur de Coucy (fourteenth century). Musée Municipal, Soissons.

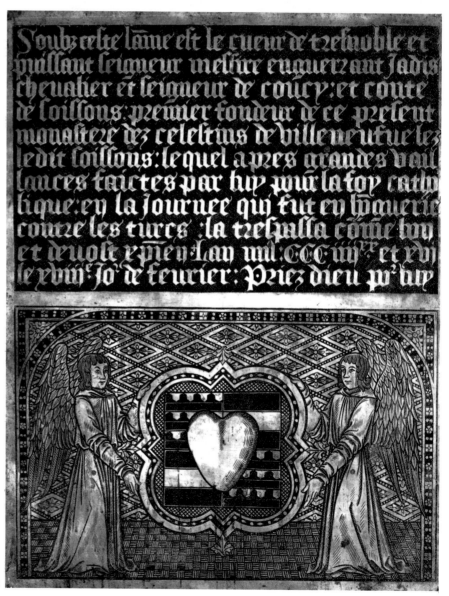

198

increasingly frequent practice of entombing the body inside the church itself. Nevertheless, inhumation did not die out and its image persists. It is often depicted in books of hours (III). Although these books also develop the iconography of the funeral procession and the service conducted at the altar, they contain many representations of ceremonies of absolution in the cemetery. Such scenes are also to be found on the altarpieces of the brotherhoods, since these associations retained their former importance in charity burials—burials of the poor, who, for their part, did not pass by way of the church. That is no doubt why the common people manifested a certain resistance to the reforms which the social elite, concerned for public hygiene, tried to impose upon funerary practices at the end of the eighteenth century and which tended to treat the cemetery as a polluted area, closed to the public.

The above observations apply in particular to regions where, beginning in the middle of the medieval period, it became customary to camouflage the corpse.

In Italy, where the corpse continued to be displayed uncovered, it

Plate III: following page 96.

199. Tomb of bishop Gonzola de Hinojosa (died 1320). San Gregorio chapel, cathedral of Burgos. See also 152a and 152b.

EXIMIA TANDEM QVA VIXIT PIETATE
OBIIT SEXAGENARIO MAIOR M DCLXXIII
SAVVS S·R·E·CARD·PATRI OPTATISSIMO P.

PETRO MILLINO IVR CON COMITI PALA
TINO OMNIBVS HONORIBVS VRBIS EX
ORDINE AC PLVRIBVS LEGATIONIBVS
SVMMA FELICITATE ET SAPIENTIA FVNCTO
CELSVS ET MARIVS PIE PARENTI
B · M · P
HIC PATRIE AMICIS NATVRE AC SVPERIS
QVE DEBVIT AD EXTREMVM VSQ PERSOLVIT
VIX AN LXXVII M II D XXI
AN D M CCCC LXXXIII XII KL APRILIS
MORITVR

200. Tomb of cardinal P. Mellini (died 1483). Church of Santa Maria del Popolo, Rome.

would be exhibited as described above but at the place of burial, not before the altar—at least, that is what is suggested by a number of curious tombs of the fifteenth and sixteenth centuries. However, one cannot help wondering whether these examples are not simply imaginary artistic simulations: in both situations, there would have been a certain psychological pressure at work.

Let us consider the tombs of Santa Maria del Popolo in Rome. The deceased is displayed on a stretcher whose poles have been removed (200); the sculptor has represented the pegs with which it was put together. The stretcher is placed either directly upon the open sarcophagus or else on the concave side of the lid, which balances on the sarcophagus rim thanks to four brackets, two of which are visible (201). I suspect—although one cannot be sure—that this incongruous arrangement is no reproduction of reality, that it is more likely an expression of a desire to use the prestige of art to maintain the illusion of displaying the body at a time when the custom was disappearing and, simultaneously, to assimilate the exhibition of the corpse to the traditional representation of the recumbent figure.

One strange episode interrupts the apparent continuity that connects the past with the present through the shifts in the climactic moments in the funeral rites and itinerary. It consists in the reintroduction of prac-

132

tices assumed to belong to a long-past paganism, followed by the disappearance of these practices in an equally inexplicable fashion. In recent excavations, archaeologists have discovered, in tombs of the thirteenth century and even later, objects arranged close to the body or propped up against it. Such objects are clearly visible in illustrations 203 (southern France, thirteenth century) and 204 (Senlis, beginning of the sixteenth century). It is a truly amazing sight!

The Musée Carnavalet contains a collection of small perforated vessels which may have contained coals (202) or incense. The vessels were found inside tombs, but they can also be seen near the body in a scene depicting the funeral of a son of Saint Louis (206).

Archaeologists from Aix-en-Provence, during excavations of various burial sites, unearthed a number of fine objects which were exhibited in Sénanque in July 1981 (205a, 205b). What did these vessels contain? What did they signify?

It is initially tempting to believe that they indicate a continuation of the pre-Christian rituals in which offerings were made to the dead, like Charon's toll. But offerings of this kind had already disappeared by the early Middle Ages, and it was only after a hiatus of several centuries that a comparable custom reappeared, in its turn to disappear in the sixteenth century or later.

This is a case worth mentioning: it provides an example of customs not to be found in any text, customs belonging to a world that is not the world of writing. They certainly did have some significance, one that the literate elite, even while tolerating them, preferred to ignore and one that today eludes us.

201. Tomb of cardinal Bernardino Lonati (early sixteenth century). Church of Santa Maria del Popolo, Rome.

203

202

204

205a

205b

206

202. Terracotta vase (thirteenth century), height 13.5 cm. Excavations at Saint-Pierre-de-Montmartre. Musée Carnavalet, Paris.

203. Grave with funerary offering (thirteenth century). Excavations at La Gayole, Var.

204. Grave with funerary deposit (early sixteenth century). Church of Saint-Pierre, Senlis.

205a. Glass gourd (fourteenth century), height 13.7 cm. Chapel of Saint-Pierre, Cannes.

205b. Glass chalice (twelfth or thirteenth century), height 9.6 cm. Papal palace, Avignon.

206. Bas-relief from the tomb of Prince Louis, eldest son of Saint Louis (c. 1260). Musée Carnavalet, Paris.

From the middle of the medieval period and throughout a great many years, there thus seems to have developed a tendency to reduce the symbolic significance of the burial—a tendency that waxed and waned, depending on the time and place.

In the nineteenth century, however, that tendency was evidently reversed. The entombment regained all its importance both in religious burials, which accounted for the majority, and in secular burials, which continued to be rare.

This happened as a consequence of the new place that the cemetery had assumed in the sensibility of the age. In a drawing by Courbet (207), we see the whole community gathering round the open tomb, as formerly it had gathered in the bedroom of the dying man until the family took its place.

207. Gustave Courbet, *Burial at Ornans.* Musée des Beaux-Arts, Besançon.

4. The beyond

Images can convey better than any texts (save those of the liturgy) how much our representations of the beyond have changed, notwithstanding our tendency to believe that these representations were fixed at a very early date.

Images also have the power to suggest the intimate and secret correspondence between, on the one hand, ideas of what happens after death and, on the other, man's consciousness of the self and of others, or the other. It is this relationship, one never explicitly formulated, that I would now like to trace through the documentary evidence.

The first scene that we encounter follows from the deathbed scene of Chapter 3. The body remains in the bed, but what of the soul? It leaves the body, taking the form of a little, naked, asexual being which is borne respectfully up to heaven in a cloth held by two angels (208, 212). Sometimes they deposit the soul at the feet of the Virgin, who has interceded on its behalf (209).

In some cases, no distinction was made between body below and soul above. The entire being — *Homo totus,* body and soul together — was seized and carried aloft by the angels (210). Such images indicate the ambiguity which for some time persisted between the fundamental unity of the being and the separation of its two constituent elements at the moment of death. Liturgical language often uses the word *spiritus,* or *anima,* to refer to "the being."

Such are the facts, often repeated. The best comment on this iconography comes from the ancient prayers of the pre-Carolingian liturgy for the dead, the *Subvenite:* "Come, saints of God, come, angels of the Lord, take his soul and carry it unto the sight of the Almighty."

But do the the souls of the dead go directly to the foot of God's throne, at the heart of his kingdom, as is suggested by fourteenth-century images in which the buildings of celestial Jerusalem appear above recumbent figures on tombs and above saints in stained glass windows? For a long time it was thought that they stopped somewhere else on the way. At first it was believed that the dead were deposited in collection places, waiting areas *(receptacula, habitacula, promptuaria)* assimilated by Saint Ambrose to the many mansions that Christ knew existed in his Father's house. Ever since Adam, the generations of the Old Testament, the prophets and the early Fathers, had been in one of these places, waiting for Christ to come and deliver them. He did so between his death and his resurrection. The place where they waited was known as hell, but this meant only the place of the dead, which was subsequently closed forever (211).

There were other places, too, which common belief confused under the name *refrigerium,* or Abraham's bosom. There are liturgies that specify: "They repose [there] until the day of Resurrection; and then forevermore, in the ages of ages, they will behold the face of the Almighty, in the company of the saints and the perfect" (cited by D. Sicard).

The dominant theme is that of waiting, repose, or sleep, just as it appears first in the language of epitaphs and, later, in the attitude of the recumbent figures (Chapter 2). This period of waiting was rejected by learned theologians — for the last time in 1334 — but the memory of it

Universa fraternitas

209

139

Preceding pages:

208. Mural dedicated to Saint Thomas-à-Becket and attributed to the Master of Espinelvas. Church of Santa Maria, Tarrasa, Catalonia.

209. Virgin with Child and, at her feet, the soul of a deceased (fourteenth century). Musée des Augustins, Toulouse.

210. Recumbent figure of a bishop (late thirteenth century). Gassicourt, Yvelines. See also illustration 73.

survived not only in the disposition of recumbent figures but in other documents of the twelfth and thirteenth centuries. In Byzantine ivories and iconostases, Abraham is represented sitting at the doorway to paradise, with souls on his knees or clustering round him like children.

Abraham's little antechamber, a relic of the past, is found again in the great period of Romano-Gothic sculpture. The patriarch is frequently depicted holding, in his lap, souls that are still wrapped in the cloth in which the angels of the *subvenite* carried them aloft (213a). Memories of the old waiting chambers may have inspired the first representations of the limbo for children who died unbaptized. The place was depicted as a closed cavern—seen, for example, in the retable of Villeneuve-lès-Avignon, which dates from the mid-fifteenth century (213b).

This belief in an interim place of rest can be explained both by the influence of the Judeo-pagan idea of a neutral place where the dead continued to live a diminished kind of life, and by the popularity of a text that foresaw an end to time and believed it to be imminent—namely, the Apocalypse according to Saint John. His description of the last coming of Christ is the one that affected men's imaginations most strongly. It inspired the first great specimens of monumental iconography, the images carved on church tympana for the faithful to behold. A good example is found at Moissac (214).

Heaven descends to earth, which it dissolves and absorbs. But where are the men who at this point were supposed to emerge, restored to life, from their tombs (215)? At Moissac, there is no sign of them. This is because their fate had already been sealed at the first resurrection reserved for the just, which had taken place one thousand years earlier and which gave rise to the concept of millenarianism which for so long stirred religious speculation.

Perhaps it is just such a first resurrection that is depicted on a sarcophagus at Jouarre, modeled on the ascension of the Savior (216). Both the risen and the Apostles raise their arms heavenward to welcome Christ, who is descending among them, holding the scroll of the book of life.

The damned are not present. They certainly exist—Saint Matthew,

140

211. *Christ in Limbo* (Germany, fifteenth century). Musée des Beaux-Arts, Lyons.

141

212

213a

213b

among many others, mentions them; but at first their presence is very discreet, or has been effaced. They are excluded from the field of the image just as they are from the memory of men and of God. Only the elect remain, not as individuals but as a composite mass, there being no need for particular judgments to distinguish among them. It is enough that they belong to the body of the saints. All that lives on in each being enters en masse into the Kingdom. The individual is absorbed into the immense family of Adam, redeemed and saved.

We have thus arrived at an idea of the beyond which combines a cosmic expansion of heaven with a gathering of the human race: the *universa fraternitas.*

Toward an individual biography

Beginning in the thirteenth century, as our gallery of images shows, this collective and massive conception of the world gave way to another representation, this time stemming from Matthew 25, in which the individual, in place of the species as a whole, became the center of the drama.

It all started with the juxtaposition of the two scenes which, though complementary in the texts, had been kept apart and isolated by sentiment and custom.

Above was the Second Coming and descent of Christ in his oval of glory, surrounded by stars. Below was the resurrection of the dead and their separation according to the only two destinations that remained for them, paradise and hell. The bosom of Abraham had become no more than an allusion, and there was as yet no purgatory (see the tympana of Beaulieu and Conques).

Next, the apocalyptic vision of Christ in all his glory disappeared, and the upper space was filled by a scene more directly connected with the one below. The new scene on the upper level was the Last Judgment (217).

The end of the story came with a sentencing, seen in illustration 217 at the most solemn moment of the verdict. Christ presides over a court of justice, like a king. At his feet an acolyte, the archangel Saint Michael, weighs the vices and virtues of the resurrected individual who stands before the court. The judge is about to pronounce sentence, but he will not follow the verdict of the scales implacably. Two advocates, the Virgin and Saint John, who kneel on either side of his throne, beg for mercy while behind them the whole celestial court prays.

Later, as literacy and the practice of writing spread, the instrument used by the archangel was replaced — or complemented — by a more abstract kind of scale, an individual balance sheet. In a fresco at Albi, each of the resurrected has an account book hanging from his neck like an identity docket (218).

In making this transition from the Second Coming to the Last Judgment, we have passed from a general view of man as a species — the family of Adam and Eve — to an inventory in which each individual soul is an object of examination and the entire life is taken into account.

Another phenomenon also made its appearance during this period: the expansion of hell. In the earliest representations, on the most ancient Byzantine icons, hell had figured only very discreetly. Between the thirteenth century and the sixteenth, it expanded and acquired greater diversity, becoming a vast and many-faceted world. The discretion of the earlier representations appears to have stemmed from the fact that the principal punishment of the damned was their extinction,

212. Two angels bearing away the soul of a bishop (fourteenth century). Musée des Augustins, Toulouse.

213a. Abraham, in a detail from the Last Judgment (thirteenth century). Central portal of the cathedral of Bourges. See also illustration 217.

213b. Enguerrand Charenton, *The Crowning of the Virgin* (1453– 1454), detail. Musée de l'Hospice, Villeneuve-lès-Avignon, Gard. See also illustration 238.

214. Tympanum of the church of
Saint-Pierre (twelfth century).
Moissac, Tarn-et-Garonne.

215. Resurrection of the dead, as
depicted on the tympanum of the
church of Sainte-Foy (twelfth
century). Conques, Aveyron.

216. Sarcophagus, Jouarre crypt
(seventh century). Seine-et-Marne.

215

216

217. The Last Judgment (thirteenth
century). Central portal of the
cathedral of Bourges.

146

their loss of being. Beginning in the thirteenth century, in contrast, men's consciousness of being became such that it affected the whole of the beyond, and during this period they no longer imagined that their being could be diminished, even in hell. Man was condemned to remain himself throughout all eternity, with all his senses and his own particular arrogant, greedy, or lascivious personality. This is why, from the thirteenth to the sixteenth century, hell and the Last Judgment remained one of the themes most often represented at church entrances and also in miniature (219). What is more surprising is to find it on a tomb, such as that of Inés de Castro (220), where one might have expected the image of hell to be considered out of place. Beginning in the sixteenth century, the center of interest moved from the judgment scene, which became less prominent, to extravagant representations of paradise and, especially, hell. The representations of hell by Van Eyck, Breughel, and Hieronimus Bosch incorporated all of the grotesque and frenzied visions invented by the fertile imaginations of the age.

Even if the Last Judgment concerned the lives of individuals, it took place once and for all, at the end of time.

Considered in the context of our film on the variations of the beyond, it appears as a compromise between the universalist and communal ideal of the early Middle Ages and the individualism of the later period.

Beginning in the thirteenth century, this individualism took another step forward, as seen in the iconography of the fourteenth to sixteenth centuries.

The Last Judgment was now confined either to imposing architectural representations or to the imaginary context of a genre painting. It was increasingly excluded from the province of the newer and more common style of piety. Its place was taken by an individual judgment, in the very bedroom of the dying man — "at the hour of our death," as it is phrased in the second part of the *Ave Maria,* composed during this period.

Little printed books were beginning to circulate among a wide public, competing with the older books of hours. They were called *artes moriendi* ("arts of dying") because their purpose was to help the sick prepare for death. They were not aimed solely at the literate. Even the illiterate could follow the sense, for they contained as many engravings as commentaries (in Latin). Like good comic strips, the engravings were self-explanatory. In illustration 221 God, heaven with its angels, and hell with its devils have all come from their cosmic dwelling places, filling the bedroom of the dying person and clustering around his bed.

Was judgment to be brought forward to the moment of death in the form it would have taken at the end of all time? Not exactly. The powers of the judge have changed. Like those resurrected at the Last Judgment, the dying man certainly has his whole life in review before him; but it is not that life, the life completed and fixed, that is about to be judged. Nothing is yet decided, not only because of the intercession of the saints, but above all because the dying man is submitting in his last moments of lucidity to a final test, whose every development we follow in detail. First come the minor temptations of anger and resentment against those who have shown him loyalty and devotion (222); then, more seriously, the temptations of despair or, conversely, of pride (vainglory) which assail him just at the moment of his last panoramic

218. Resurrected souls carrying the books of their lives, as seen in a detail from *The Last Judgment* (early sixteenth century). Cathedral of Sainte-Cécile, Albi.

219. Illumination from the *Heures de la duchesse de Bourgogne* (fifteenth century). Musée Condé, Chantilly.

220. Tomb of Inés de Castro (died 1355). Alcobaça, Portugal.

220

221 to 225. Illustrations from an *Ars moriendi* (fifteenth century). Bibliothèque des Arts Décoratifs, Paris.

225

view of his life. The devils whisper: "You don't have a chance; you are lost; the best you can do is commit suicide" (223). Or they flatter his vanity: "You have nothing to fear, no cause to repent; you have led an exemplary life; you deserve the victor's crown" (224). In each scene, the angels offer the opposite view, but it is left to the dying man to choose freely, and heaven and hell lean anxiously toward him to find out what he will do. The outcome of this test will determine his eternal fate. In the case of our particular *ars moriendi,* he will be saved. God the Father has lowered the arrow that he holds in his hand. He has pronounced death, deliverance for the candidate, now that the trial is over (225). Death and deliverance is now confused with a judgment that was formerly put off to the end of all time.

The scene retains the familiar features of the deathbed scene (see Chapter 3): a priest places a candle in the dying man's hands, and the angels of the *subvenite* come to collect the man's soul (221). All that used to take place at the end of time now happens at the hour of death, in conjunction with the traditional rites—no longer in the explosive world of the Apocalypse but instead in an existing and private place, the bedchamber, at the bedside.

The point is that God appears not so much as a judge but rather as an arbiter whose task is to determine the result of a test. Man holds his destiny in his own hands. He is given advice by the angels and devils and encouraged by the prayers of the angels; but it is he who decides, and the decision depends upon his last reactions at the threshold of death. This iconography is characterized by the freedom of the dying

151

226. *The Death of the Sage*
(woodcut, Burgundy, seventeenth
century). Bibliothèque Nationale,
Paris.

man. Its clerical character is weakened, and it acquires a new element
of pathos: death is the moment when each man intuitively recognizes
his entire life, which is illuminated suddenly as by a flash of lightning
and revealed to him in every detail.

This iconography persisted from the sixteenth century to the present
day, but it eventually developed into a series of illustrations of the good
death and the bad. The existential and pathetic content that moves us in
the pages of the *artes moriendi,* whether we be believers or not, disappeared in the eighteenth and nineteenth centuries, giving way to a
crude onslaught of clerical propaganda directed in particular against
unbelief.

As early as the seventeenth century, the invasion of the dying man's
bedroom by the worlds of above and below disappeared. Each quietly
returned to the place assigned to it by ecclesiastical conformism (226).
Free will, man's power over himself, which the medieval *artes* showed
man to possess when faced with death, yielded to the faithful and flat
illustration of a dogmatic treatise.

To judge by a seventeenth-century engraving, a mere handful of messengers from heaven now sufficed (226). Saint John the Baptist is still present, but the guardian angel, a new creation of the Counter-Reformation, has taken the place of other intercessors. Most striking is the fact that the priests — reading prayers and sprinkling holy water — have become the principal actors. In a lithograph dating from the first half of the nineteenth century (227), even the remaining celestial mediators have departed, and the priest, on his own, replaces them; it is he who puts the decisive choice before the dying man, pointing with one hand to heaven, with the other to hell.

A comparison of two documents, one from the fifteenth century, the other from the nineteenth, makes it possible to gauge how much meaning has been lost in the interval.

The fifteenth-century miniature (229) shows a wicked rich man going to hell. Despite his fate, the scenes of his life and even of his death retain a naïve vigor, even a spontaneous attractiveness, which arouse as much pity and regret as they do condemnation.

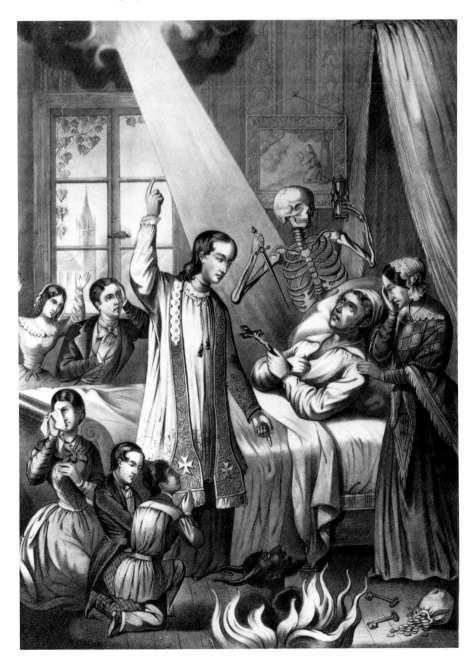

227. *The Dying Man Prepared to Meet God* (mass produced in Metz, nineteenth century). Bibliothèque Nationale, Paris.

228

228. *Individual judgment* (late nineteenth century). Color illustration for a mural catechism, printed by La Bonne Presse. Private collection.

229. *The Deaths of the Rich Man and the Poor Man* (Strasbourg school, fifteenth century). Musée de l'Oeuvre Notre-Dame, Strasbourg.

230

231

230. Recumbent figure (fifteenth century). Former abbey of Saint-Vaast, Arras.

231. Illumination from the *Miroir de l'humaine salvation* of Vincent de Beauvais (fifteenth century). Bibliothèque Nationale, Paris.

232. *Death with an Hourglass* (Strasbourg school, sixteenth century). Musée de l'Oeuvre Notre-Dame, Strasbourg.

In the (mass-produced) posters with which the priests of the nineteenth century placarded their mission buildings, nothing is left of this ambiguity. All that is visible is a determination to convince at any price, even at the cost of vulgarity (228).

The comparison between these two images shows how a theme becomes impoverished once it ceases to express a fundamental anxiety and turns into a weapon of propaganda.

The sudden recognition of one's life, which we have discovered beneath the symbolism of the *artes moriendi,* is found in a more emphatic and pathetic form in the macabre art of the fourteenth to sixteenth centuries. But here it was a matter not so much of one individual life but of "life" in general, in all its most attractive aspects.

It is customary to use the word "macabre" to describe an iconography that was frequent but *not dominant* (particularly in a funerary context) during this period, and in which the principal figure is a *transi*—that is, a decomposing corpse inhabited and gnawed by worms, with shreds of flesh hanging from it. Sometimes this figure is stretched out like a reclining figure on a tomb (230); it is precisely what the recumbent figure underground is in the process of becoming. At other times, it is a personification of death—less an allegorical character than a supernatural agent that has taken the place of the angels and devils to execute the decrees of God (231). God delegates his powers to death and entrusts him with the arrows of death and the documents that identify the condemned. The engravers of the *artes moriendi* filled the bedroom with visitors from earth, heaven, and hell; in contrast, the very presence of the macabre figure of death causes the room to empty (168).

Death is truly a figure of this period, during which people learned to tell the time: he keeps his eyes fixed upon his ever-present hourglass (232). He shows scant respect for the traditional periods of respite and gives little warning: his victims barely have time to react. On the walls of cemeteries (Les Innocents in Paris) or of church-cemeteries (Meslay-le-Grenet), the *danse macabre* gathers in its train rich and poor and young and old alike (233, 234).

Their faces are still free to express surprise. Not so, however, for the victims of the Triumph of Death—one of Petrarch's "Triumphs"—a kind of charnel house on the move which crushes its victims before they are aware of it (235).

But the macabre figure of death is not simply an agent of destiny combining and concentrating in one symbol elements that used to be separate and diffuse. He is not altogether on the side of God, whose decrees he executes, nor of Satan, whose realm he fills. He communicates with a hidden world which, in the fifteenth and sixteenth centuries, he helped reveal: a world that emerges from the depths of the earth and from the interior of the body, inhabited by worms, toads, snakes, hideous monsters—a teeming fauna produced by corruption; a world of deformities that still haunted the relatively late visions of Breughel and Bosch but that imaginative historians such as P. Camporesi have also detected in the vermin of the seventeenth century. The physicians of the seventeenth and eighteenth centuries set out to destroy that fauna, or at least to tame it.

How did such a radical iconography emerge—the counterpart to the beyond of both the Last Judgment and the individual judgment?

232

157

233

234

233 and 234. *Danse Macabre*
(fifteenth century), fresco.
Meslay-le-Grenet, Eure-et-Loir.

Most historians interpret it as a manifestation of the traumas that people suffered during the plague epidemics of the fourteenth and fifteenth centuries. I personally hesitate to accept this view, although I agree that the numerous deaths in densely populated areas may well have provided disturbed imaginations with the model of the *transi,* the visible sign of great terror. For my own part, I believe that this iconography reflects not so much the very real misfortunes of the times, but rather an excessive attachment to life. The greater the passion for life, the more painful the bitterness of being wrested from it.

The *artes moriendi* had certainly seized upon the dying man's fury at having to leave his house, his orchards and gardens, the wines in his cellar, and his relatives and friends (236). Man now took his revenge for the inevitable separation by substituting for a world loved to the point of passion its reverse — a world of vermin and chthonic monsters. That is what death is.

This transition from the desirable to its hideous reverse is well conveyed by the myth of the tempter, as represented in Strasbourg or Fribourg-en-Brisgau. Satan offers Eve the apple (237). From the front, he seems to have the attractive form of a young and graceful scholar, a figure frequent in fourteenth-century art. But from the rear, a rent in his back reveals a seething mass of disgusting creatures that live within. Seen from the front he is life; from the back, death.

Purgatory

We have now traced two major thematic tendencies in representations of the beyond. Each in its own way testifies to a correspondence between the idea of a beyond and the idea of man himself, considered sometimes as an element inseparable from a collective destiny, sometimes as a unique and complete individual, master of his destiny to the last.

In the sixteenth century, these great surges of feeling seemed to be exhausted; the medieval iconography seemed to do no more than repeat itself, had lost its inspiration, had become detached from its roots.

The fact is that as early as the eleventh and twelfth centuries, something momentous happened which quite upset the topography of the beyond. It was the discovery of purgatory, whose history has been skillfully traced by Jacques Le Goff. Purgatory had certainly always existed in Christian thought. It was a place for errant souls that had managed to escape damnation but whose faults barred them from sharing the repose of the "saints." They suffered tortures that resembled those of hell, and they "returned" as ghosts (or, as the French say, *revenants*) to beg for the pity and prayers of the living. It was the duty of the living to anticipate such a fate and make sure that endowments were set up to pay for services and Masses in aid of their sinful souls.

But it was the logic of the twelfth and thirteenth centuries that reorganized the beyond to accommodate these souls in distress and allotted them a definite place of purgation. Purgatory superseded the gathering places for waiting and repose that had figured in the archaic eschatology, and also the locations — scattered through this and other worlds — where those sentenced to finite periods of torture endured their punishment.

From our own point of view — namely, that of the iconography — what is striking is the long dearth of images. Jacques le Goff has noted a few miniatures in fourteenth-century books of hours in which the essentials of the theme already appear, but that does not amount to very

Preceding page:

235. Illustration from Petrarch, *The Triumph of Death* (1503). Bibliothèque Nationale, Paris.

236. Woodcut from an *Ars moriendi* (fifteenth century). Bibliothèque des Arts Décoratifs, Paris.

237. *The Seducer* (fifteenth century). Cathedral of Strasbourg.

236

much. The real ancestor of the iconography of purgatory remains a painting that is found today in the charterhouse of Villeneuve-lès-Avignon; it depicts the crowning of the Virgin and dates from the second half of the fifteenth century (238). Until that period — and on the whole even until the late sixteenth century — purgatory was absent from the iconography, despite the fact that in Dante's *Divine Comedy* it occupies a place of importance equal to those of hell and paradise.

In the context of our study, such an absence is as significant as an abundance of images. Notwithstanding the arguments put forward by Jacques Le Goff and Pierre Chaunu, I see no way to interpret this silence except as a resistance (though certainly not a conscious one) prompted by the idea of a period of repose and expectation — an in-

238. Enguerrand Charonton, *The Crowning of the Virgin* (1453–1454). Musée de l'Hospice, Villeneuve-lès-Avignon, Gard.

stinctive unwillingness to turn the interim period into one of tortures, and a natural preference for punishments of a milder and more picturesque kind. Be that as it may, the problem that is the most striking and that raises the most questions for us, as image seekers, is the veritable explosion of purgatories in the iconography of the seventeenth century and their extraordinary success in the popular piety of the eighteenth, nineteenth, and early twentieth centuries. In Catholic countries, the souls in purgatory have become the most familiar of the denizens of the beyond.

As Michel and Gaby Vovelle have shown, virtually every church has an altar consecrated to "the souls in purgatory," an altar whose up-keep is the responsibility of a special brotherhood. These altarpieces

239

239. *The Souls of Purgatory*
(eighteenth century). Church of
Saint-Nicolas-du-Chardonnet, Paris.

240. Jean Daret, *Purgatory*
(seventeenth century). Church of La
Madeleine, Aix-en-Provence.

243

241. Plate from a mural catechism, printed by La Bonne Presse (late nineteenth century). Private collection.

242. Diploma dated 1691, issued by the brotherhood of the Ames du Purgatoire (Souls of Purgatory). Private collection.

243. A charnel house in Naples.

faithfully reproduce an iconography that constitutes the popular image of the beyond for Catholics of the period.

The souls, in the form of their earthly bodies, are represented as surrounded by flames but not suffering great pain, and in attitudes of prayer with their arms raised toward heaven, which they sense but do not yet see. The devils of Villeneuve-lès-Avignon have, for the most part, disappeared: purgatory is now run by angels. The latter provide the souls with refreshment by pouring water down to them from small vessels (241), and deliver them from their torments to introduce them to God's bliss (239).

I believe that the popularity of purgatory can be accounted for by two, related, phenomena.

One is a change in its meaning: purgatory ceased to be a temporary hell, reserved for a few great sinners saved *in extremis,* and became the antechamber to heaven through which all the elect, with the exception of the canonized saints, had to pass.

244. Gomberville, *The Doctrine of Mores,* or *Man Is Nothing but a Bit of Mud* (eighteenth century). Private collection.

245. Pierre Subleyras, *Charon Ferrying Shades over the Styx* (eighteenth century). Musée du Louvre, Paris.

The other is a change in sensibility which began to render intolerable the departure of loved ones. In the early stages of this development — corresponding to the wide diffusion of the idea of purgatory — it was the place where those who had passed away went and where, until one joined them, one communicated with them through prayer. Thus, among the souls depicted in purgatory by the painter Daret, Michel and Gaby Vovelle have identified his son, represented at the moment when an angel is carrying him off to heaven (240). Daret thus assured the salvation of his child, whom he hoped one day to join in paradise.

Something barely detectable in the seventeenth century became accentuated in the eighteenth and nineteenth centuries. The real subject of the image ceased to be the place, purgatory, and became the relationship established between the living and the dead, thanks especially to the ancient institution of Masses for the deceased: every such Mass despatched a contingent of souls to paradise, so the duty of the newly elect was to manifest their gratitude (241). Special brotherhoods organized these exchanges. In this way, their members ensured that spiritual aid would be forthcoming after their deaths, and they received diplomas that confirmed their privileges (242). The dialogue between

246

the two worlds had become a means for the poorest in the community to save the only possession left to them—their own identity.

An Italian anthropologist, Patrizia Cambelli, has written of the customs that persist even today in Naples (243): "Every Monday, hundreds of people [now disapproved of by the clergy] come to the underground cemeteries of the churches [the charnel houses, where they select and adopt a skull] to embark upon a symbolic voyage to the dead. They come from the poorest classes and bring with them offerings of flowers, candles, coins, and other small objects; in exchange, they request mercy and protection from the souls in purgatory . . . They transfer to the dead their need to save their own identities, which were in danger of being effaced in the life eternal. By establishing a reassuring relationship with these souls, they seek to preserve their own historical memory once they have passed on into the life eternal." This is an important text which underlines the connection between the existence of purgatory and the affirmation of personal identity.

It is perfectly logical that the souls in purgatory should no longer have to return to earth: they replaced the ghosts *(revenants),* for whom there was no longer any *raison d'être.*

And yet, there still were ghosts. They ceased to take the form of *transis* or skeletons, nor did they have their earthly bodies, which they preserved in purgatory. They reappear in the eighteenth century as mysterious figures concealed in shrouds—like the specters being ferried by Charon in the painting by Subleyras (245), or the shades that haunt the crypt-porticos of Gomberville, strewn with skeletons and broken bones (244), or, eventually, the veiled, disembodied figures of nineteenth-century funerary statuary (246, 247).

These later ghosts seem to occupy a new, intermediate space, dark and cold—that of a *roman noir*—created by the imagination of the eighteenth and early nineteenth centuries. It replaced, or complemented, purgatory as a place of transit until the concept of a great meeting of memories superseded it, in the nineteenth century.

The place of reunions In the nineteenth century emerged an important phenomenon which, in its early stages, coincided with the success of purgatory. As we shall see in Chapter 7, it became extremely tempting to see the beyond as a place for reunion, for rediscovering earthly affections, following the interval of trials between the deaths of spouses.

In Christianity this was a new sentiment, although it had occasionally been expressed earlier in images of resurrected spouses emerging hand in hand from the tomb; or in paintings in which tender hearts, in the tradition of Saint Francis (Fra Angelico, for example), see paradise not only as a place for the conversation of saints seated in majesty but also as a garden full of flowers where friends spiritually reunited could walk together in pairs, hugging each other in their joy (248).

Christianity had inherited Old Testament prohibitions against recalling the dead and, besides, there was no popular pressure in favor of such a practice. It was up to each individual to take out some form of insurance in the beyond, and to ghosts in distress to manifest themselves.

As sensibilities became more demanding and links between the living and the dead became less collective and more personal, purgatory provided a good compromise between the Old Testament prohibitions and the pressures of the developing affectivity. (This was a

246 and 247. Funerary sculptures in the cemetery of Nice.

248. Fra Angelico, *The Last Judgment* (c. 1430), detail. Convent of San Marco, Florence.

247

248

249. *Purgatory* (late nineteenth century). Bibliothèque des Arts Décoratifs, Paris.

250. William Blake, *The Soul Hovering above the Body* (early nineteenth century). Bibliothèque des Arts Décoratifs, Paris.

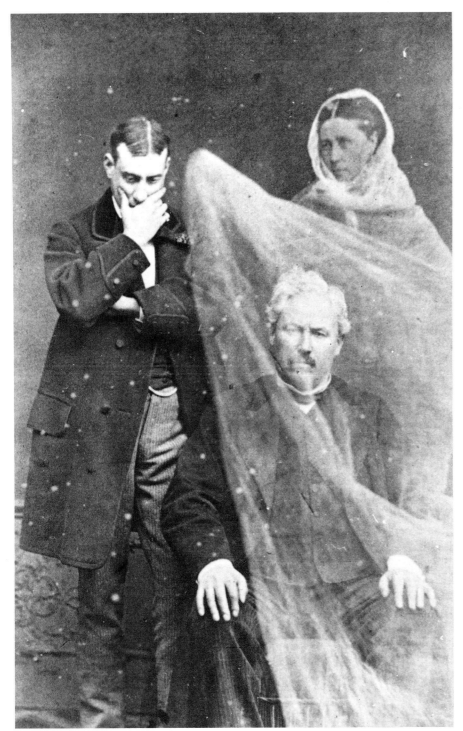

251

251. Apparition in a faked photograph (c. 1865). Private collection.

252. Apparition in a faked photograph (c. 1855). Académie de Médecine, Paris.

252

253. Lithograph (1840).
Bibliothèque des Arts Décoratifs,
Paris.

174

compromise consistently rejected by Protestant creeds, which, ever since Luther, had been opposed to any concessions to the dead.) Illustration 241 bears expressive witness to the ancient but increasingly exalting relationship between the Mass, the intentions of the living, and the fate of the dead.

However, beginning at the end of the eighteenth century, communication between the living and the dead no longer depended either on the Church, with its three-tiered beyond, or on the vestiges of popular beliefs that were a distant legacy of pagan animism.

Closer relationships between the living and the dead, which I believe were responsible for the great popularity of purgatory among Catholics, also developed outside the churches, in positivist and even anticlerical milieux. This was a tide that swept the entire Western world, regardless of religious allegiances.

It produced two, only slightly different, attitudes. The first was that of the Catholics: they either brought purgatory closer to paradise, as can be seen in illustration 249 (the festival of 2 November), or else dispensed with purgatory altogether. For the dear departed, there was no longer a hell or a purgatory — only a home for tender earthly relationships reconstituted in eternity.

The second attitude was that of the nonbelievers, of whom there were many in the anticlerical milieux of the early nineteenth century. For them, what remained after death was not the soul posited by philosophers or Christians but a physical being, an astral body (250), which could even leave its impression upon a photographic plate when it responded to the appeals of the living (251, 252).

Even when the afterlife was not proven scientifically in this fashion, it became confused in people's imaginations with memories of the dead, producing an illusion of reality. Thus, a painter of 1840 catches the presence of a mother who has died in childbirth and has returned to see her child and pray at its side (253).

It is understandable that this naïve belief in a beyond of reunions should be evoked insistently and precisely by funerary iconography, yet be spurned by other forms of art and by religion itself. Consider, for example, a tomb in the cemetery in Nice (254): a little girl, dressed in her Sunday best, welcomes her brother to the beyond (here, the paradise of Christians), running to meet him with outstretched arms.

254. Garino tomb, by A. Frilli (1925–1930). Cemetery of Nice-Gairaut.

5. Omnia vanitas

Up to this point our photographic sequence has, like an uninterrupted genealogy, carried us with no break in continuity from the early Middle Ages to the seventeenth century and even a bit beyond.

But now we come to a new sequence, which overlaps with the preceeding one. It begins as early as the sixteenth century.

The temptation of nothingness

We seem to be entering a very different world—we must turn the page and look ahead.

From the very first images, it is obvious what is happening: we are crossing a frontier and coming upon a new sensibility. Death has changed its place and its meaning. Let us see how this has happened.

Actually, there has not been time for all the themes themselves to change; but how differently they are treated! Violence, fear, and sexuality now invade a domain in which life and death have become inseparable.

Recall the macabre image of death which prevailed in the fifteenth century (Chapter 2). That decaying, worm-infested figure retained a lordly air, taking his time and going about his business with a slow, triumphant step. A simple gesture was enough to convince his victim, who was scarcely at all surprised, already resigned.

At the end of the sixteenth century the *transi* was replaced by a clean, dry skeleton relieved of the sordid humors of the body and the earth. This was quite a different character. He no longer marched as if in a parade but ran, leaped, flew, perpetually in motion. He was not of the earth or heaven or hell. He had an indefinable world of his own, a theatrical world in which he was the principal, indeed the only actor.

In the paintings of Baldung Grien (257) he looms up behind his prey—here a young mother who is as yet quite unaware of his presence, as is her horrible fetus. Death fixes his insect eyes upon them; his face is split in a grin of satisfaction.

In sixteenth-century woodcuts (255, 256), death's task seems less easy. He needs all the strength he possesses to tear from their despairing families a woman and a small child, who are only too aware of what is going on. Whatever their age, they resist with all their might.

As he passes on his way, the nimble skeleton seizes without compunction whatever perverse pleasures have been left behind by the inhabitants of the beyond. Shamelessly, he gropes lasciviously up the skirts of a young woman he has called for: the abduction becomes rape and violation (258, 259).

Here is a new theme which pervaded Western art until the twentieth century, particularly in the Germanic and Scandinavian countries, albeit not always with the same eroticism and violence. In these works, death offers the opportunity for an otherwise impossible love affair. The theme is that of death and the young girl (261).

A late medieval tradition depicted death entering a public place in the course of a banquet and discreetly selecting his victim there, unseen by the other, unsuspecting guests. What did this scene become in the baroque period? In a late seventeenth-century painting (260), the skeleton abruptly interrupts a card game, disguising neither himself nor his intentions. At the sight of him, the horrified players, their eyes popping out of their heads, fall over backward and flee.

255

256

176

255 and 256. Hans Holbein the Younger, two woodcuts from *The Dance of Death* (1538).

257. Hans Baldung Grien, *The Young Woman and Death* (sixteenth century). Musée d'Art Ancien, Brussels.

258. Nicolas Manuel Deutsch, *Death and the Young Woman* (1517). Kunstmuseum, Basel.

259. Hans Baldung Grien, *The Knight, the Woman, and Death* (sixteenth century). Musée du Louvre, Paris.

260

260. *Players Surprised by Death* (southern Italy, late seventeenth century). Musée du Berry, Bourges.

261. Adolf Hering, *The Young Girl and Death* (c. 1900). German postcard, private collection.

In all these scenes, with their well-known themes, the new element is eroticism — and in most cases violence, of which eroticism is but one aspect. The former master of ceremonies has become a hunter of humans, and, in changing roles, he has also changed his form. The skeleton belongs to a new space in which the sensibilities of the future were to take shape; it is an imaginary space halfway between the natural and the supernatural, between what can be seen and what is no longer either visible or invisible but believed in with as much conviction as if it were a matter of positive realities. The skeleton is the principal figure in this imaginary world. He rules unchallenged over baroque imagery.

His origin — but not that of his extraordinary success — is scientific: he was born from the development of anatomy in the sixteenth and seventeenth centuries. Science in those days was not limited to a small elite. It provided the occasion for social and fashionable entertainment. A lesson in anatomy, like the defense of a thesis, was more than a demonstration reserved for initiates — it was a social event worth recording. People would have their pictures painted grouped around a

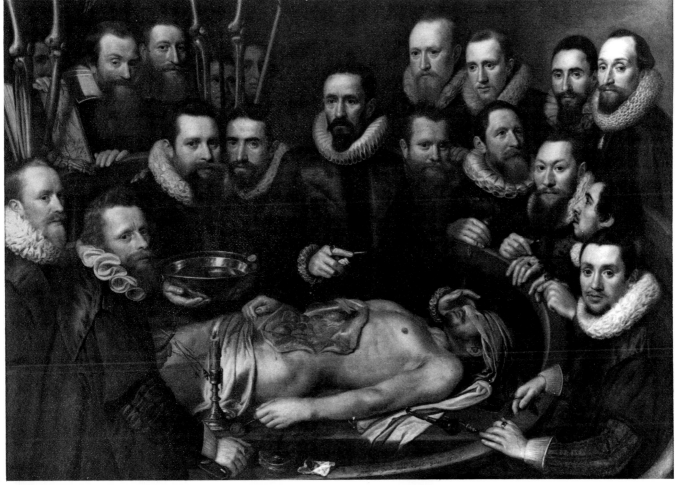

263

265

Surgite mortui venite ad Judicium

262. Thomas de Keyser, *Doctor Sebastien Egbertsz's Anatomy Lesson* (1619). Historical Museum, Amsterdam.

263. Pieter Michielsz van Miereveld, *Doctor W. van der Meer's Anatomy Lesson in Delft* (1617). Municipal Hospital, Delft.

264. Illustration by André Vesale from *De humani corporis fabrica* (1543). Bibliothèque des Arts Décoratifs, Paris.

265. Illustration by Jacques Gamelin from *Nouveau recueil d'ostéologie* (Toulouse, 1779). Bibliothèque de l'Ancienne Faculté de Médecine, Paris.

dissection table, just as they would around a banquet or card table or at a musical concert.

Illustrations 262 and 263, both extremely imposing paintings, show two groups of worthy Dutch bourgeois, the first group posing around a *skeleton*, and the second around an opened *cadaver*. The dead body with its layers of veins, muscles, and bones aroused no revulsion in people of that time—particularly since, beginning in the sixteenth century, the vermin of the late Middle Ages would have been eliminated, leaving cadavers cleansed and—as we should say today—sterilized. Indeed, they provoked a strange curiosity inspired as much by fantasy as by science, a curiosity that art sought to express. An anatomical preparation such as Dr. Fragonard's horseman (preserved at the veterinary school of Alfort) was regarded as an *objet d'art*, just like a sculpture. Science, death, and a kind of fascination combined to inspire a coherent iconography not unlike the comic strips of today.

Anatomical illustrations, treatises on osteology, and even manuals on horsemanship, which set out to demonstrate objectively how the body worked, superimposed the imaginary upon reality and created a fascinating world of dried up mummies and skeletons. The skeleton is not simply a collection of bones; it lives, moves, and bustles about in both popular engravings and scientific works. There is something disturbing and surprising about the need to turn it into an animated being.

This being sometimes assumes the pose of an Arcadian shepherd by Guercino or Poussin, and contemplates a skull placed on a tomb (264). Elsewhere he emerges from the earth on a day of resurrection that is no longer for the flesh but for bones (265).

The figure of the skeleton is characterized not only by his visible bones but also by a whole group of imaginary associations whose expression is concentrated in his mouth and eyes.

His mouth is always open in the grimace that we would today call a "rictus" (257). The word did not exist in those days. It appeared at the beginning of the nineteenth century and originally denoted the movement imparted to the mouth by any kind of laugh. But it was not long before the meaning became limited to the grin of a baroque skeleton, a toothless old man, a madman, or a corpse affected by rigor mortis. This grimace was an invention of the baroque period and was described at the time as "sardonic," which was a newly invented word—more than just a word, a physiognomic category, if not a veritable state of soul. *Sardaine* is a type of root whose effects were described by an Italian author in 1544 (cited by P. Camporesi): "Those who die from having eaten it look like a person laughing." The *sardonic* laugh is the laugh of the skeleton. It remained so for as long as art continued to use the skeleton, as in the "decadent" painting of Belgium and Germany at the end of the nineteenth century and the beginning of the twentieth.

The second characteristic trait of the baroque skeleton is his gaze, or what takes its place, giving him the air of a being from another world. The gleaming shadows in his eye sockets resemble the huge eyes of some creature from another planet, like the extraterrestrials of our modern comic strips.

Once he had stepped out from the scientific illustrations where he originated, the skeleton enjoyed a remarkable success in baroque iconography. Certainly, the *transi* had never known such popularity. The skeleton replaced the *transi* in the traditional role of a *memento mori* in the preacher's pulpit (266), at the foot of cemetery crosses (267),

266. Skeleton preaching (sixteenth century). Velez chapel, cathedral of Murcia, Spain.

267. Tomb at Marville, Meuse.

266

267

268. Funerary medallion of Thomas
de Marchant et d-Ansembourg and
his wife, Anne Marie de Neufonge
(died 1728 and 1734). Church of
Tuntange, Luxembourg.

and in small portable tokens (279) even as late as the early nineteenth century in America (350).

He came to hold a new place in the paraphernalia of death, one that, with the aid of a number of baroque tombs, we must now attempt to interpret.

In the first example, a German tableau of the early eighteenth century designed to be hung on the wall (268), skeletons have clearly taken the place of the dead, but in the anonymous bones there is nothing left to render the people recognizable; their individuality, their physiognomic features, have disappeared. All that remains in this assembly of bones is the allegory of a couple: two spouses leaning tenderly toward each other, clinging together so as to yield as one to the movement that is sweeping them away. The husband embraces his wife, who clasps her bony hands in front of him in a gesture of both prayer and protection. It is an isolated scene in a depersonalized dance of death where all the distinctive features of the dancers have been effaced. In this dance of bones we can detect a sentiment that is characteristic of the late Middle Ages: the agony of losing everything. And there is another, too, one that heralds preromanticism: the desire to hold fast to an immortal love.

On another tomb, in the church of the Santi Apostoli in Rome (269), even the skeletons have not withstood the wear and tear of time. They have fallen apart and the pieces are stacked up in a heap in a charnel box resembling a sarcophagus. They might well have spilled out had not the angel, who is contemplating them in some perplexity, decided to raise the lid. Whatever can he be going to do with all these separate pieces? Nothing? Hardly. For, like a new Ezekiel, he is clearly intending to put them together again: the pyramid nearby provides an assurance of immortality.

In both these cases the personality of the deceased has disappeared, to be replaced by the familiar skeleton, either an animated or a dismembered one.

The other tombs that are shown here express a more dramatic opposition between life and nothingness, or the nothingness of life and blessed immortality. The composition of Giovanni Battista Gisleni's tomb in Santa Maria del Popolo is very simple (270). It is divided in two by the epitaph. Above it is a portrait of the deceased. He looks very much alive, but the inscription tells us that he is not alive (not "no longer" alive). Below is a skeleton behind an iron lattice. His arms are crossed in the traditional attitude of the recumbent figure, and he is wrapped in a shroud that leaves his head visible: it seems quite clear that this is the dead Gisleni in his coffin. However, the inscription sets us right: *this* Gisleni is not dead.

It is all illusion: the man who is truly dead looks alive, while the skeleton lives. But the latter is not alive in earthly appearance; he lives by virtue of the death that has transformed him into a creature of bones.

The next two tombs reproduce a model that was common in Bernini's time in Rome, Naples, and indeed the whole of Italy. In the first, the skeleton, winged like an angel, appears to be emerging from an open tomb, flourishing a painted or sculpted portrait of the deceased which he is no doubt carrying off to heaven (271). What makes the skeleton fly in this way? Where is he going? Who is he? Despite all his agility, he represents none other than the wear and tear of earthly existence, as is proved by the fact that on another tomb, one of a

269. Tomb of Maria Lucrezia Rospigliosi Salviati (died 1749), by Bernardino Ludovisi. Church of the Santi Apostoli, Rome.

symmetrical pair flanking a church entrance, he is replaced by the figure of time in the guise of an old man (272).

One is struck by the opposition between the skeleton and the living man he is carrying off. Once again, where is he taking him? To a beyond where life continues, or to his own nothingness? The question is a crucial one, yet the answer is not immediately apparent. Does the triumph of death now mean the triumph of nothingness? It is tempting to suppose so, but we know that such an interpretation is not in keeping with the pious climate of the Counter-Reformation. All the same, a slight unease, if not a doubt, persists, as if nothingness were taking the place of the devil. In that case, might the skeleton be a mixed creature, on the model of an androgynous being — half winged angel, half sardonically laughing devil?

The Altieri tombs in the church of Santa Maria in Campitelli, in Rome, display with schematic simplicity the two contrary tendencies of the age (273, 274). On the one hand, they adopt the traditional model of the sequence of great medieval examples seen in Chapter 2, while, on the other, their classical style avoids any baroque extravagance. These tombs are situated on two lateral walls of a family chapel, facing each other, on either side of the altar. Each comprises two levels. The lower ones are taken up by two large cenotaphs, their only ornament a word engraved in huge gold letters: *nihil* on the man's monument, *umbra* on the woman's. It would be hard to devise a drier statement of the nothingness of life. After life, is there now only shadow and nothingness? It would seem so. God appears to be dead. But moving on, we discover above these disturbing cenotaphs two familar and reassuring traditional praying figures, kneeling and seen from the front. The woman holds a missal in her hands, while the man, hand on heart, turns toward the altar to follow both the Mass that is being celebrated there and also, beyond it, Christ's Mass in paradise.

On the tombs carved in the manner of Bernini, nothingness and immortality were juxtaposed in an ambiguous fashion so that, from a naïve reading of the message, one was not sure which of the two would win out. On the Altieri tombs, in contrast, the meaning is quite clear: immortality is superimposed upon nothingness and the former overcomes the latter. Such a contradiction, more or less satisfactorily resolved, is a commonplace in Roman epitaphs of the seventeenth century. One of them (in the hospital of San Onofrio) reads like an epitaph to nobody: "To Sir Nemo: life is no longer anything after death; his assurance and delight lie in life in heaven."

The Middle Ages laid emphasis on the risks of a life that was too full. With melancholy and bitterness, the baroque sensibility registers the fact that life is empty. Only God and religion can fill the void. But if faith falters, the world that it can no longer restrain veers off in the direction of nothingness, which has always exerted such a pull on it.

272

270. Tomb of Giovanni Battista Gisleni (died 1672). Church of Santa Maria del Popolo, Rome.

271. Tomb of Alexandro Valtrino (seventeenth century), by Bernini. Church of San Lorenzo in Damaso, Rome.

272. Tomb of Giulio del Corno (died 1662), by Ercole Ferrata. Church of Gesù e Maria, Rome.

273

It sometimes happened that the skeleton and his companion, the desiccated corpse, moved out of the world of the imagination to places that were not reserved for the social elite (as were dissection amphitheaters and church tombs) — namely, to the crypts of the most popular cemeteries of the time, those of the Capuchin monasteries. All of a sudden, or almost, and in contradiction to a tradition that in the West went back virtually a millennium, it was no longer deemed desirable to conceal the body in the earth or take it out only as loose bones to be piled in charnel houses. Attempts were made to preserve it in its entirety, in its clothes, by using techniques derived from embalming or mummification or from the preparation of bodies for anatomical dissection, and to exhibit it in the form of a mummy or skeleton.

Several cemeteries of mummies are still in existence. One of the most interesting is the Capuchin cemetery in Rome (275). It is situated neither outdoors nor in a church but down in a cellar. The eighteenth-century monk who masterminded this creation used the bones that had piled up over the centuries in the church's charnel houses to produce a theatrical or operatic setting. By arranging shoulderblades here and tibias there, he constructed all kinds of architectural patterns and furnishing: niches, columns, lamps. In illustration 275, a skeleton suspended from the ceiling holds in his hands the scales of the Judgment, also composed of bones.

274

VMBRA

Jean-Jacques Bouchard, a French traveler who visited southern Italy in 1632, described the tomb in Gaeta of the *connétable* de Bourbon (commander of the imperial army that sacked Rome), who died in 1527: "Through the first door that you come to after passing the guard-house, [you see] the place where de Bourbon is: it is a little recess cut in the thickness of the wall, closed with wooden bars. Over the door, on either side, there are two quite long inscriptions, one in Spanish, the other in French . . . Having opened the first door, you open a large cupboard in which stands de Bourbon, upright on his feet . . . The flesh still covers him so completely that you can recognize all the lineaments of the face and the eyes, which are open. The chin and lower jaw are somewhat spoiled . . . But the body is quite whole, and the balm that the Spaniards had him given when he died has preserved the flesh so well that even after five hundred years it retains its shape and color, except that it is a bit dark, dry, and hard. He seems to be extraordinarily large."

Treating the body after death was, of course, alien to conventional Western practices. In the East, however, it was embalmed and kept aboveground; and at least one artist, Carpaccio, envisaging the circumstances of entombment in the Orient, painted a landscape full of mummies as well as bones (277). With spectacles such as that in the de Bourbon vault, one could find a similar mingling of the dead and the

273 and 274. Tombs of Angelo Altieri and his wife, Laura Carpegna, by Mazzuoli (1709). Church of Santa Maria in Campitelli, Rome.

191

275

living. The imagination was doubtless stimulated to consider the Resurrection—when the soul would reunite with and truly reanimate the body (276, 278).

We know that the type of display found in Capuchin vaults remained customary for many years in Italy, right to the mid-nineteenth century in Palmero. The personalization of the visible skeleton corresponded both to the devotions paid to the souls of purgatory, and to the new desire to pursue the dialogue beyond death.

Homo bulla In the society of the sixteenth and seventeenth centuries, symbols of death were not restricted to the places particularly reserved for them (cemeteries and oratories, for example); they also decorated objects used in daily life. People would wear them in the form of rings, brooches, and pendants (279).

Families would distribute such ornaments of mourning to those who attended the burial of one of their members. The "death's head" thus became a common decoration that was worn on the hat or engraved on one's watch, when the first fob watches made their appearance (287).

We are certainly justified in interpreting these objects as *memento mori* with nothing particularly original about them, in the tradition of the late Middle Ages. That is what they indeed were. But they no longer, as in the old days, invited the beholder to repent lest he be overtaken by death: now they also expressed the sentiments of modern man in the face of the nothingness that he was in the process of discovering.

Those sentiments provided the inspiration for a new genre which was given the highly significant name of "vanities," a reference to the phrase from Ecclesiastes frequently cited at the time: *Vanitas vanitatum et omnia vanitas.* Vanities were, in effect, still lifes. But since the end of the fifteenth century, the genre had been expressing a taste for life and nature, a passion for things and their appearances. Men had always delighted in representing certain objects for the sake of the love they inspired and the joy to be derived from contemplating them, touching them, embellishing them through the techniques of art. Suddenly we find these things caught by the painter at the evening hour, when they are losing their freshness and sinking toward their decline: worn books with still legible pages that suggest the vanity of life and the proximity of death.

The familiar objects of the genre assume a new symbolism: candles flicker, pipe smoke curls away, music fades, flowers wither, butterflies flutter for the last time, glasses fall and are shattered, bread grows stale, weapons rust, all things decay. New objects are introduced, and these provide the key: the skull (often in association with a portrait), the watch (sometimes in pieces—it no longer tells the time), the hourglass. The symbols spell out the message: death lies within all living things (280, 281, 282, 283). Soap bubbles float in the air, a child's game but also an image of man: *Homo bulla,* runs the Latin proverb, a common formula that appears in all kinds of allegories of life (that is to say, of death). We see this in the painting of the anatomy lesson in Leyden (284), where skeletons surround the dissection table, brandishing banners on which can be read all the commonplaces of the period: *Homo bulla, Memento mori, Pulvis et umbra sumus, Mors ultimum, Vita brevis, Nosce te ipsum.*

Art is determined to track down the illusion that lies beneath appearances. The Burgkmaier spouses see their own skulls when they look in the mirror (285). The scene combines two illusions—that of old age and that of the reflection; but the reflection is truer than the reality.

This theme made a lasting impression on men's imaginations and was taken up again by the decadents of the late nineteenth century (many of whom we can recognize as the heirs to the macabre and the baroque). The mirror certainly reflects the image; but, in an anamorphosis, subject and image both fade away and the mirror itself, together with its reflection, changes into a death's head (286). An anamorphosis by Holbein the Younger likewise expresses the hidden presence of death within life: the skull is hidden at the center of the picture and becomes detectable only when seen from a particular angle (287). In contrast, in illustration 288, the severed head of Charles I reveals, in a cylindrical mirror, a bust of the king when alive.

In order to perceive the hideous creatures that inhabited the tempter of Strasbourg (237), it was necessary to walk right around him; a single

275. First underground chapel of the church of Santa Maria della Concezione (known as the Capuchin chapel), Rome.

278

276. Engraving by Agostino Veneziano after a design by Rosso Fiorentino (Italy, 1518). Bibliothèque Nationale, Paris.

277. Carpaccio, *Entombment.* Staatliche Museen Preussischer Kulturbesitz, West Berlin.

278. Luca Signorelli, *Resurrection of the Flesh* (1499–1504), detail. Chapel of the Madonna de San Brizio, cathedral of Orvieto, Umbria.

279. Pendant of the Elizabethan period. Victoria and Albert Museum, London.

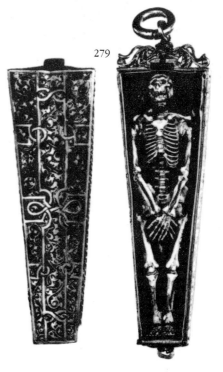

279

280. *Vanity,* after Philippe de Champaigne. Musée de Tessé, Le Mans.

281. *Vanity* (seventeenth century). Musée du Louvre, Paris.

282. S. Renard de Saint-André, *Vanity.* Musée des Beaux-Arts, Lyons.

283. S. Renard de Saint-André, *Vanity.* Private collection.

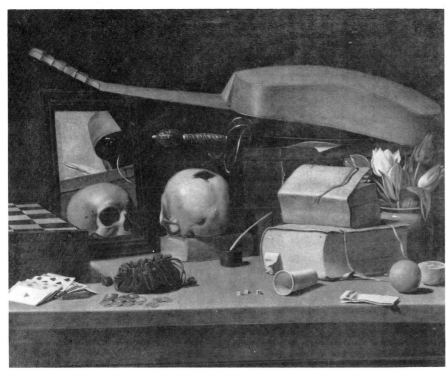

281

283

glance could not encompass both the elegant façade and the foul interior. In contrast, in the seventeenth-century engraving shown in illustration 289, one passes smoothly through an invisible erosion from body to skeleton. The covering of flesh simply becomes transparent; no actual change takes place. Which is more real, the covering or the frame beneath it?

The story of life merges with that of death: this is the lesson conveyed by an engraving of 1647, a quite unexceptional work with no artistic pretensions and a moralistic purpose which, alongside an almanac, might well have adorned the home of an ordinary artisan (290). The legend adopts the commonplaces of vanities and epitaphs. There is the usual contradiction: "what nurtures [man] consumes and extinguishes him"—he is a smokey wisp of nothingness, like the candles of the vanities. It is an extraordinarily spare message, devoid of any religious content. The sun sets in a night without hope: it is the *umbra* of the Altieri tomb (274) and of the slogans in the Leyden amphitheater (284).

In a world designed to deceive the eye, death is the secret of life; but it is a secret that hides nothing—nothing but nothingness.

In all fairness, we have no right to remove these engravings and vanities from the walls where they hang alongside other images, pious ones, of Virgins, crucifixes, and saints. Nevertheless, the two domains remain separate. God could fill the void, but for him to become present in the life of men, the latter had first to create a void.

Still—what if God happened to withdraw, even for a moment? Illusion would regain all its powers, and the only way to encompass it would be to accept the stark reality of nothingness.

It is therefore not surprising that the spirituality of the period—and the iconography that was quick to express it—tended to see life as close to death, in accordance with the old Pauline tradition, now given new overtones.

That is why I would situate here, despite their early date (end of the fifteenth century), the *Triumph of Life* and *Triumph of Death* that Lorenzo Costa painted in the chapel of a church in Bologna (291, 292). He treated the subject in a spirit closer to that of the sixteenth and seventeenth centuries than to that of the end of the Middle Ages or the Renaissance. Already, this *Triumph of Death* no longer shows the ground strewn with corpses. Its interest lies above all in the comparison drawn between the two allegories. Each comprises two levels: below, the allegory of the triumph and, above, illustrations that are much more unusual.

At their lower levels, the two triumphs resemble each other: one could exchange them without really noticing. It is at the upper levels that the differences become apparent. Death reveals a paradise in which a soul is arriving, welcomed by two angels; life, in contrast, is symbolized by a kind of globe crammed with scenes of misfortune.

The most striking thing is not the traditional Pauline paradox of the upper levels, but rather the nearly identical lower levels of life and death and their respective allegories.

The fascination of the corpse

Now let us return, as in a cinematic flashback, to the anatomy lessons in illustrations 262 and 263. The former, with a skeleton for its subject, led us first to the theme of the sardonic, then toward nothingness. The

latter, centered on the opened cadaver, introduces another series of images which we should now explore.

Beginning in the sixteenth century, a new theme appeared in portrait painting: the realistic representation of a man (or a woman) recently dead. The eyes have been closed and the body lies on a bed prior to being transferred to a coffin. Such scenes (which were to become extremely frequent in the art and photography of the nineteenth century; see Chapter 7) were apparently born of a desire to represent not just a person but a dead person. The portrait was used not only to preserve the features of a living person, but to fix them in death. It is as if death gave him an extra measure of personality. Most of the portraits in our collection come from northern Europe. One is that of a thirty-six-year-old woman (293). An inscription in Flemish that runs round the frame tells us that she was born on 21 December 1532 at three o'clock and died on 12 January 1568: "May God have mercy on her soul." The inscription resembles an epitaph.

Similar portraits are attributed to Rembrandt and Rubens.

These works, few in number, do not include many men or members of the laity; the custom appears to have been mainly reserved for nuns.

285. Lucas Furtenagel, *The Burgkmaier Spouses* (1529). Kunsthistorische Museum, Vienna.

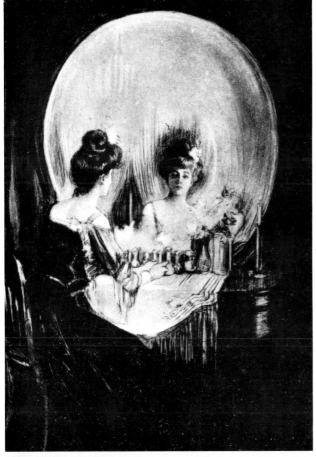

288

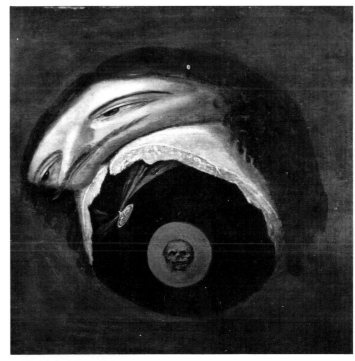

286

287

286. Illustration by Charles Dana Gibson, from a German postcard (c. 1908). Private collection.

287. Hans Holbein the Younger, *Ambassadors Jean de Dinterville and Georges de Selve* (1533). National Gallery, London.

288. Anamorphosis, *Charles I of England* (English school, c. 1660). National Museum, Stockholm.

However, we do possess one portrait of a canon of Cambrai who died in 1563: this, too, bears an inscription reminiscent of the epitaphs on many tombs (294).

In the Hospital of Saint-Jean in Bruges, a number of portraits of nuns have been preserved: they are represented in a solemn pose, clasping a parchment (probably the diploma of their vows), their heads crowned and their arms adorned with foliage (an interesting detail). Next to the bed, a candle burns (295). In all likelihood, these portraits were destined to be hung in a hall or gallery in the convent.

We should include in this series the portraits of dead children, also painted as they lie in bed, which began to appear in the seventeenth century. One example is a striking portrait by an unknown artist in the museum of Besançon (296). It was in just such a realistic form that little children who were not princes had been represented, wrapped in swaddling bands, on the earliest tombs to be devoted to them (297).

There is something new about these portraits of corpses: religious symbols and emblems are either absent or very discreet. The portraits must have been intended for private, cloistered places inside convents or homes.

The memory of the living person was thus preserved in the form of his or her corpse. The realistic corpse, quite different from the imaginary medieval *transi* and the baroque skeleton, both of which bore no resemblance to the subject, now appears as a mode of representation and deserves a place in our story.

Until the sixteenth and seventeenth centuries, and even much later among the working classes, death was confined by society to restricted areas or ghettos. In those days it was encountered only in churches, tombs, books of hours, and other such places.

With the sixteenth century came an important change whose effects are still being felt today. Death emerged from its lair, insinuating itself here and there in domains formerly proscribed to it. Gradually it came to be found everywhere, as can be seen from the vanities mentioned above.

The corpse that was barely cold, the body almost or completely dead but not yet disfigured by decomposition, became an element of genre painting as well as of portraiture. But the path to this point was neither simple nor direct. It followed strange and twisted detours, passing through a land of torture and eroticism. There were, no doubt, many feelings of reticence to be overcome before the dead could be represented as truly dead. In anecdotal art prior to the fifteenth century, there is nothing to distinguish a dead person from a living person, unless the former has some weapon sticking into him or has been chopped in two with an axe.

The first attempt to indicate death realistically consisted in rendering pallor—the *pallida*. Examples are the Christ child in Bellini's *Madonna of the Meadow* (298) and the chalk-faced woman in Baldung Grien's portrait (IV).

In the fifteenth and sixteenth centuries, realism was further pursued. Many genre scenes betray a fascination with death where, not many years earlier, efforts would have been made to attenuate or minimize it. Thus, no compunction was felt in representing the infant Jesus on the Virgin's lap no longer as a child playing with fruits or birds or seeking his mother's breast, but as a little corpse, a prefiguration of the Passion (299).

Plate IV: following page 96.

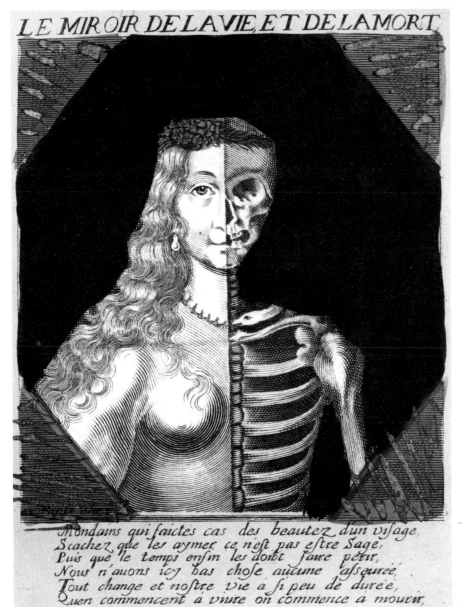

LE MIROIR DE LA VIE, ET DE LA MORT.

Mondains qui faictes cas des beautez d'un visage.
Scachez que les aymer, ce n'est pas estre Sage,
Puis que le temps enfin les doibt faire perir,
Nous n'auons icy bas chose aucune asseurée,
Tout change et nostre vie a si peu de durée,
Qu'en commencent a viure on commence a mourir.

289

289. *The Mirror of Life and Death*
(seventeenth century). Musée
Carnavalet, Paris.

290. Illustration from Francis Bacon,
The Story of Life and Death (1647).
Bibliothèque de l'Ancienne Faculté
de Médecine, Paris.

Overleaf:

291 and 292. Lorenzo Costa, *The
Triumph of Life and of Death*
(1489). Bentivoglio chapel, church
of San Giacomo Maggiore, Bologna,
Emilia-Romagna.

290

294

293

295

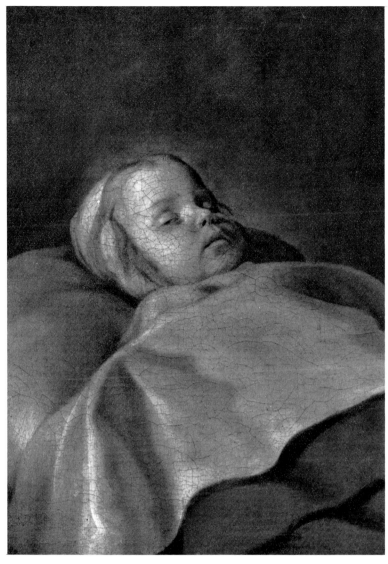

293. Funerary portrait (sixteenth century), by Barthel Bruyn the Younger. Musées Royaux des Beaux-Arts, Brussels.

294. Portrait of canon Gery Balicque (died 1563). Palais des Beaux-Arts, Lille.

295. Portrait of Sister Barbara Godtschalk (died 1698). Hôpital Saint-Jean, Bruges.

296. *Dead Child* (northern school, seventeenth century). Musée des Beaux-Arts, Besançon.

297. Tombstone in the church of Munshausen, Luxembourg.

298. Giovanni Bellini, *Madonna of the Meadow*. National Gallery, London.

299. Parmigianino, *Madonna with the Long Neck*. Uffizi Gallery, Florence.

300. Urs Graf, *The Devil and the Lansquenet* (1516). Kunstmuseum, Basel.

Now a new alliance was forged between death, violence, suffering, and sex, one that was to affect the Western imagination until the surrealist period and even beyond. It is an extraordinary innovation, indicative of quite a different aspect of the contemporary sensibility.

At the beginning of the sixteenth century, the relation between death and sex (which we have already encountered in the myth of the young girl and death) took the form of obscenity: genital caresses (258), or a display of testicles—for example, by Dürer's horse of the Apocalypse or the devil as depicted by Urs Graf (300). In the seventeenth century, however, the sexuality was masked, in many cases unconscious, and we have to wait for the *libertinage* of the eighteenth century, the obsessions of the nineteenth, and the psychology of the twentieth for it to break through the mask once again.

Mystic ecstasy resembles a scene of death as much as a scene of love; this is a point that has often been made in connection with Bernini's saints, and it was one that was perfectly apparent to the French eighteenth-century travel writer, the *président* de Brosses. The similarity is to be found on other, less well known tombs—for example, that of Aurora Bertiperusina in the church of San Pantaleon in Rome: she contemplates the altar, both hands on her breast as if to contain her heart, like either a woman in love or one who is dying.

The torments of the martyrs provide another meeting point between death and desire. Although the naked bodies of the martyrs and the Caravaggesque gestures of their tormentors may originally, in all innocence, have been imputed to piety, it is clear to us that they betray a delectation close to that described by the Marquis de Sade a century later—of which they are, in fact, the origin. Examples abound: the flaying of Saint Bartholomew, the roasting of Saint Lawrence, the martyrdom of Saint Victor (301), the corpse of Hector dragged along by Achilles. It is not just the suffering of the naked corpses that arouses desire but, more generally and in a more diffuse and subtle manner, the softness of these bodies which life has only just abandoned and death has not yet stiffened. They are exquisite images, whose langor and sensuality are—consciously or not—lovingly and lingeringly rendered by the artists. Consider, for example, Rosso's Christ, Rubens's Saint Stephen (302), Poussin's Adonis, and, finally, Bigot's Saint Sebastian (V), who is dying under the ministrations of Saint Irene without its being terribly clear whether he is succumbing to his wounds or her caresses.

The conjunction of death and desire gave rise to a new category of eroticism. At first diffuse and barely detectable, it was confirmed at the end of the eighteenth century and the beginning of the nineteenth. It became necessary to find a name for it, and the one adopted denoted the sickly langor of bodies too tender, ambiguous; it was then extended to refer to the desirable corpse. The word was "morbid." It acquired a real aesthetic value, being understood as a variation of "the beautiful," and its effects were much sought after. The beautiful young corpse now acquired in the aesthetic sensibility a place reminiscent of that of the young ephebe in Hellenistic culture. An example is the sculpture of a young man, the victim of an assassination, by Chastel, an artist from Aix—a statue that (we are told by Michel Vovelle) was much imitated by worthy masons endeavoring to lend luster to their initiation ceremonies.

Plates V and VI: following page 96.

210

Beginning in the early nineteenth century, no compunction was any longer felt about representing love between the living and the dead — either discreetly, as in an erotic image of the death of Atala (303), or without any ambiguity, as in the embrace of the dead Hyacinth by his lover who has accidentally killed him (304).

Fuseli knew exactly what it was all about when he painted Brunhild gloating over the tortured body of the handsome Gunther (VI). This was the period of the *roman noir.* Lovers were no longer content with one last embrace before death: now they desired to break through the wall and satisfy their desire with an exhumed corpse. There are many cemetery scenes that show an open tomb and a dead girl being exhumed by a husband, lover, or father (305, 306). They no doubt belong particularly to the fantasmagoria of art and literature.

However, there were some occasions when the morbid figure crossed the frontier of reality. Until the nineteenth century and even the early twentieth, the execution of criminals remained a great popular spectacle (307). And another spectacle was added, at least for the French: the public exhibition of corpses in the city morgue. The good folk of Paris would visit the morgue just as they might stroll along the boulevards. As Jules Janin wrote: "One enters that place without thinking anything of it; the door is always open." The punctilious morality of the period made no fuss about such exposure. It was not until the twentieth century that these two great spectacles of death were concealed from the public eye: the morgue was transformed into a laboratory (although, if we are to believe J.-L. Hennig, that did not do away with all its disturbing, mysterious fascination), while the guillotine and gallows were concealed behind the prison walls.

The genealogy of the images throws a glaring light on the striking differences in our culture prior to and after the sixteenth and seventeenth centuries.

Until the seventeenth century, the two concepts of death and life with all their respective associations were kept separate. Subsequently, they destroyed and encroached upon each other. Life was now impregnated with death. Today we refer to taboos when we might more correctly speak of saturation.

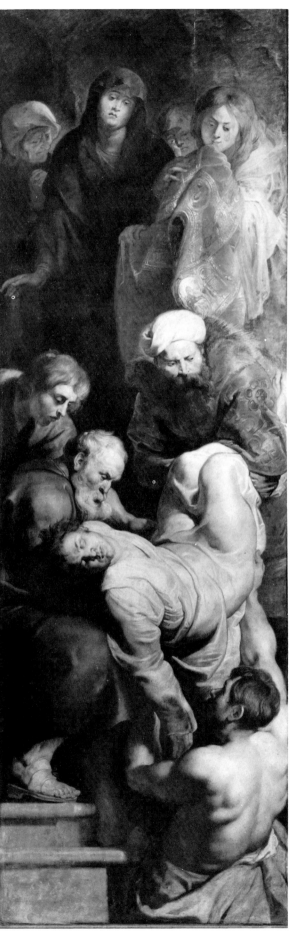

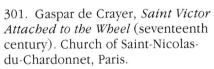

301. Gaspar de Crayer, *Saint Victor Attached to the Wheel* (seventeenth century). Church of Saint-Nicolas-du-Chardonnet, Paris.

302. Rubens, *Entombment of Saint Stephen*. Musée des Beaux-Arts, Valenciennes.

303

304

303. Girodet-Trioson, *The Funeral of Atala* (1808). Musée du Louvre, Paris.

304. J. Broc, *The Death of Hyacinth* (nineteenth century). Musée des Beaux-Arts, Poitiers.

305. P. A. Vafflard, *Young and His Daughter* (1804). Musée Municipal, Angoulême.

306. *The Madness of Love: A Man Removing His Fiancée from the Tomb* (Austria, 1897). Bibliothèque Nationale, Paris.

307

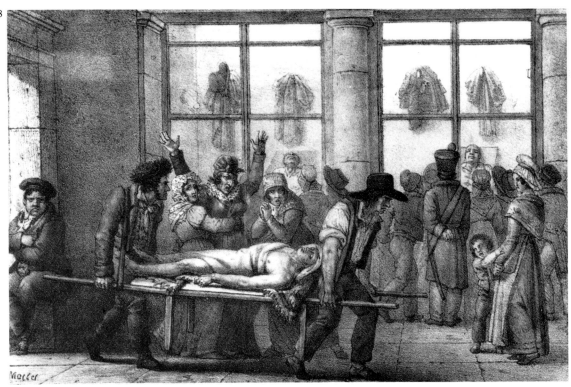

308

307. Théodore Géricault, *The Execution* (nineteenth century). Musée des Beaux-Arts, Rouen.

308. Marlet, *The Morgue* (c. 1820). Musée de la Police, Paris.

6. The return of the cemetery

At the end of the eighteenth century and in particular at the beginning of the nineteenth, a new model of the cemetery—that of our own contemporary necropolises—took the place of the charnel houses that surrounded churches from the Middle Ages to the seventeenth century, as at Les Innocents in Paris. But to understand this new transformation of the cemetery, we must turn back to consider aspects that I deliberately omitted from Chapter 1 in order to avoid obscuring the direction that developments took. The impression I gave was that there was a break in continuity between the linear cemetery (Merovingian, non-Christian) and the charnel houses of the Middle Ages. However general and significant that phenomenon may be, a number of exceptions should now be mentioned. The open-air cemetery was not everywhere absorbed by the church or reduced to a pauper's graveyard.

I suggest that there are three distinct types of open-air cemeteries: cemeteries with crosses, cemeteries with rectangular or rounded stelae, and—an intermediate case—the cloister cemetery.

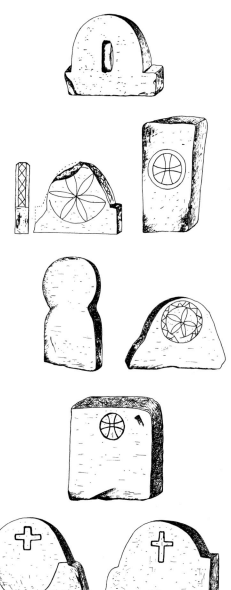

After Jacques Sirat, "Les stèles mérovingiennes du Vexin français," *Bulletin archéologique du Vexin français* 2 (1966) and 6 (1970).

The cemetery with crosses is particularly interesting because it indicates a continuity in the eschatological significance of the cross going back to the seventh century—but a subterranean one, masked since the twelfth century by the funerary trappings in churches, and reemerging only at the beginning of the nineteenth century. The model of the cross is thus, on the whole, rare and marginal. Let us attempt to trace its history.

I am assuming that we should seek the origin of the tomb cross in the Merovingian cemeteries. Recall what we noted earlier about them: stone sarcophagi, buried in shallow pits, would be topped with a stela of stone and probably also one of wood. These stelae were the only visible signs of the burial place and indicated its location. Virtually all of them have disappeared; the only surviving ones have been found reused—as sarcophagus lids, for example. A number of specimens from the sixth and seventh centuries, mainly from the Vexin region, are preserved in the museum of Guiry. The drawings reproduced here from the museum's catalogue, compiled by Jacques Sirat, give us some idea of their appearance, as does illustration 309, which shows a stela engraved with a cross still in position at the head of a tomb.

Whereas some are totally unadorned, on most there is either a kind of cavity or a rose design or a cross. The same motifs cover the walls of seventh-century plaster sarcophagi discovered in the Paris region, which are preserved in the Musée Carnavalet (310). One of these motifs is particularly intriguing, as it recalls the wooden crosses with peaked roofs found in cemeteries from the Middle Ages to the present day (317).

Let us now move from seventh-century Guiry-en-Vexin to a site further south, Usclas-du-Bosc in the Hérault. Its ancient cemetery, still in use today (like that of Marville), until recently preserved its late medieval core (probably dating from the thirteenth, fourteenth, and fifteenth centuries) consisting of rows of disk-shaped stelae whose form had already been established at Guiry in the seventh century: a carved cross within a disk, resting on a base sunk into the ground. Alongside the cross, we find the even more ancient motif of the rose design. Records

309

309. Merovingian tomb (sixth or seventh century). Brèves, Nièvre.

310. Plaster sarcophagus (seventh century) from Saint-Germain-des-Prés. Musée Carnavalet, Paris.

311a and 311b. Disk-shaped stelae from Usclas-du-Bosc. Musée Fleury, Lodève, Hérault.

311a

311b

310

217

312. Muiredach cross (tenth century). Monasterboice, Louth, Ireland.

313. Stela with shoemaker's symbols. Archeological museum, church of the Carmo, Lisbon.

313

314. Disk-shaped stela. Sare, Pyrénées-Atlantiques.

315. Funerary cross (sixteenth century). Musée des Augustins, Toulouse.

316. Funerary cross (sixteenth century) of Dame Guillemette, wife of Jean Azemar, blacksmith, who died in Toulouse during his pilgrimage to Santiago de Compostella. Musée des Augustins, Toulouse.

317. Illumination from the *Heures de Neville* (c. 1435). Bibliothèque Nationale, Paris.

314

315

316

317

show that these crosses were not planted in a random fashion, as were the monuments of urban medieval cemeteries depicted in books of hours, but were still oriented and aligned in the manner of the Merovingian rows. This layout seems to me quite remarkable, suggesting— as do the shapes of the stelae—a continuity with the cultures of the early Middle Ages, despite their very real differences. These stelae are now preserved in the Musée Fleury in Lodève (311a, 311b).

We should, then, recognize a continuity between the Merovingian stelae and the disk-shaped crosses.

It would be interesting to compile a chart showing the disposition of these crosses; it might then become apparent that they survived only in regions that were isolated or peripheral in relation to the nerve centers of Christianity. They survived in places where the open-air cemetery continued to be used by already well-to-do families of peasants or artisans—those who were no longer content with anonymous graves or ephemeral wooden crosses and wanted to mark their burial places with durable monuments, often using folk-art devices and extremely inventive traditional artistic forms. Such crosses can be found in Ireland (312), Portugal (313; note the cobbler's tools), in Basque country (314), and in Languedoc, where they were known as "Cathars." The four arms of the cross appear to have had some difficulty in disengaging themselves from the circular mass that contained them. Around the sixteenth century, however, they managed to do so. The Musée des Augustins in Toulouse contains some very fine examples in stone, dating from about the sixteenth century (315, 316)—sometimes accompanied by an inscription, possibly in the Occitan language, and displaying symbols of various trades (for example, the weaver's shuttle) or the emblems of pilgrims (such as the seashell of Saint James).

Once it had become free-standing, the cross often appeared in cemeteries depicted in the fifteenth-century books of hours, but in wood, as a simple cross reduced to its plain four arms or topped with a little protective roof (317), like those found in nineteenth-century cemeteries and in central Europe today. This type of cross was probably more common over a longer period of time than it appears. The crosses, being made of perishable materials, did not survive; and frequently, instead of being reproduced, they were replaced by other models found in the churches.

Where the cross was made of stone, it persisted for a longer time within a frame, one that would originally have been disk-shaped but that gradually changed. Thus, at Marville, there is a cross supported by large baroque scroll designs (318).

One of the most curious examples of the long persistence of the pseudo-disk-shaped cross, outside the Basque region, is to be found in the little cemetery of Schoenberg in Luxembourg (323), dating from the late eighteenth and early nineteenth centuries. Here we find solar symbols, rose-shaped stelae of the Merovingian type (322), and crosses inscribed within circles as in Languedoc, Portugal, and Ireland two or three centuries earlier. Where the stones display new symbols, these retain an early medieval flavor: a palm tree indicates the paradise to which the deceased has been called, or, as on a little stela in a neighboring cemetery, at Junglinster, it may become the tree of life (319). The cross motif is sometimes repeated a second time on the lower part of the stela, in the form of the Cross of Calvary flanked by those of the two thieves. Christ's monogram—the insignia of the Company of

319

320

321

322

323

319. Cross in the former cemetery of the village of Junglinster, Luxembourg.

320. Detail from a cross leaning against the church of Niederwiltz, Luxembourg.

321. Cemetery cross depicting a plough. Schoenberg, Luxembourg.

322. Cross inscribed "1803 T.S." Schoenberg Cemetery, Luxembourg.

323. Crosses in the Schoenberg Cemetery, Luxembourg.

324. Crosses at Bidarray, Pyrénées-Atlantiques.

324

325 and 326. Funerary reliefs at
Marville, Meuse.

327. Jewish cemetery, Prague.

326

Jesus, which was very popular in Europe during the Counter-
Reformation—sometimes fills the center of the cross. The dead who
are buried in these simple and beautiful tombs, which manifest a certain desire for sculptural expression, must have been peasants, rich
agricultural laborers; some, in fact, insisted on depicting in the corners
of the cross the instrument of their prestige and prosperity: the plough
(321). Others preferred the symbols of a baroque vocabulary: the
scythe and the hourglass, or the snake biting its own tail, a symbol of
immortality (320).

The same evolution, leading from the medieval disk-shaped cross to
the cross of the funerary symbolism of today, is again detectable in the
Basque region, as can be seen from tombs dating from the first half of
the nineteenth century, slightly later than those of the Grand Duchy of
Luxembourg (324).

These little early nineteenth-century cemeteries in Luxembourg appear to be not only the last Merovingian cemeteries but also the first
cemeteries of the contemporary period.

328. The Old Granary Burying
Ground, Boston, Massachusetts.

In the Anglo-Saxon world, the cross was strongly associated with Catholicism and it was only with the High Church revival (when the Church of England became less Protestant), in the mid-nineteenth century, that it appeared commonly in British cemeteries. By the end of the century, however, it had been adopted even by nonconformists and by the mid-twentieth century even by nonbelievers.

Indeed, for unbelievers and believers alike, the cross has become a part of the common language of our communications code, in which it signifies death. A cross displayed after a name states, quite independently from any (at least conscious) idea of salvation, that the subject has recently died.

The cemetery with crosses can be seen as either a relic or a precursor, despite the fact that there had probably always been wooden crosses in the majority of open-air cemeteries from the Middle Ages to the eighteenth century. When tombs became visible and individual, they tended to take a different form: that of a rectangular stela with a rounded top.

The most striking example is that of Marville, where the cemetery, which probably dates from the Middle Ages, has remained in use right to the present day and where quite a number of seventeenth-century open-air tombs have been preserved. Some of the stones were deposited in the church of Saint-Hilaire in the nineteenth century, but others have remained *in situ*. Even at first glance, it is evident that they correspond to mural tablets detached from church walls or pillars and, quite simply, stuck into the earth. On them we find, once more, religious

330. Headstone of David Lang, dated 1762. Blanford church, Petersburg, Virginia.

227

331

332

331 to 333. Tombstones from the cloister of Les Jacobins, Toulouse.

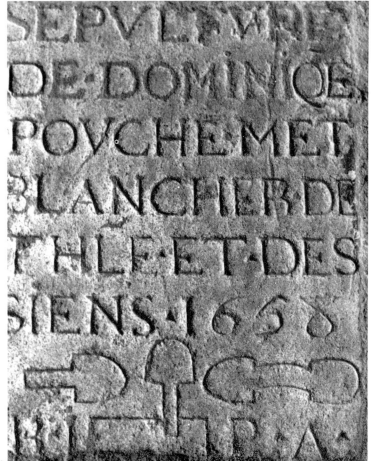

333

334

334. The letter tau, the ploughshare, and the pruning knife — details on an ancient "plague cross" (1458). Waldbremus, Luxembourg.

scenes, praying figures, sometimes a patron saint such as Saint Nicholas (325).

These are, in effect, the tombs of master craftsmen or minor magistrates — members of a municipal petty bourgeoisie which anywhere else at this particular period would have made a point of being buried inside the church. Here, however — and in this fact lies the originality of Marville — this class used the ancient open-air cemetery but brought to it monuments copied from those in the churches rather than derived from the archaic disk-shaped models. This fidelity to the old type of cemetery, generally abandoned by the upwardly mobile classes, was combined with a popular and piquant style of sculpture that no doubt originated in local workshops (326). Although this type of tomb was rare in seventeenth- and eighteenth-century France, it is prevalent wherever burial has always taken place in the open air — in Jewish communities, for instance, since there are no tombs inside synagogues (327); and also in places where, even though the practice became less common, it persisted more strongly than in continental Europe — in England, for example, or in the English colonies of America (328, 330). The English headstone derived from the same models as the stelae of Marville but became simplified, schematized, and familiar

Overleaf:

335. Graves with headstones and horizontal slabs. Marville, Meuse.

336. Skullbox next to church portal. Lanloup, Côtes-du-Nord.

337. Skullboxes in a charnel house at Marville, Meuse.

229

through frequent and constant use: it was associated with protestantism, as we have noted, and became the virtually unmistakable sign of an Anglo-Saxon cemetery from the seventeenth to the nineteenth century. In the latter half of the nineteenth century and in the twentieth, in towns at least, it lost that quasi-monopoly. But even today it has not entirely disappeared and when seen abroad remains, so to speak, a survival of Britain—for example, in a cemetery in Montreal (329).

As we have seen (Chapter 2), beginning in the late seventeenth century, in the towns, the master craftsmen and professional bourgeois were laying claim to an identity beyond death. There were many who wanted visible tombs, on which they declared their names and professions even if they declined to display other biographical data such as the exact dates of birth and death—data which, in the aristocratic or clerical milieux of the Middle Ages, had been a primary manifestation of the consciousness of the self. Only the year of death was recorded, other details being considered unimportant.

However, these artisans and merchants were not always buried inside the churches, in the noblest and most costly section of the cemetery precinct. Between the paupers' yard and the church for the rich, there were intermediate areas: the arcades of the charnel houses and cloisters. Like the church naves, these arcades were paved with tombstones, particularly in the monasteries of mendicant orders such as the Dominicans and Franciscans. Some still survive in the Jacobin cloisters of Toulouse: a ropemaker (331), a candlemaker, and so on. The inscription is sometimes decorated with a skein of ropes or a cluster of

336

337

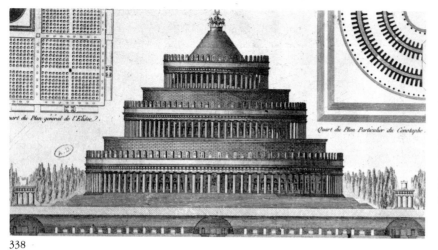

338

338. Plan for catacombs, by Jomard (1800). Bibliothèque des Arts Décoratifs, Paris.

339. *Campo Santo of the Hospital of Santo Spirito,* painted mock-window. Vatican Library, Rome.

340. Gallery of arcades in Staglieno Cemetery, Genoa.

341. Drawer-like niches in Staglieno Cemetery, Genoa.

339

340

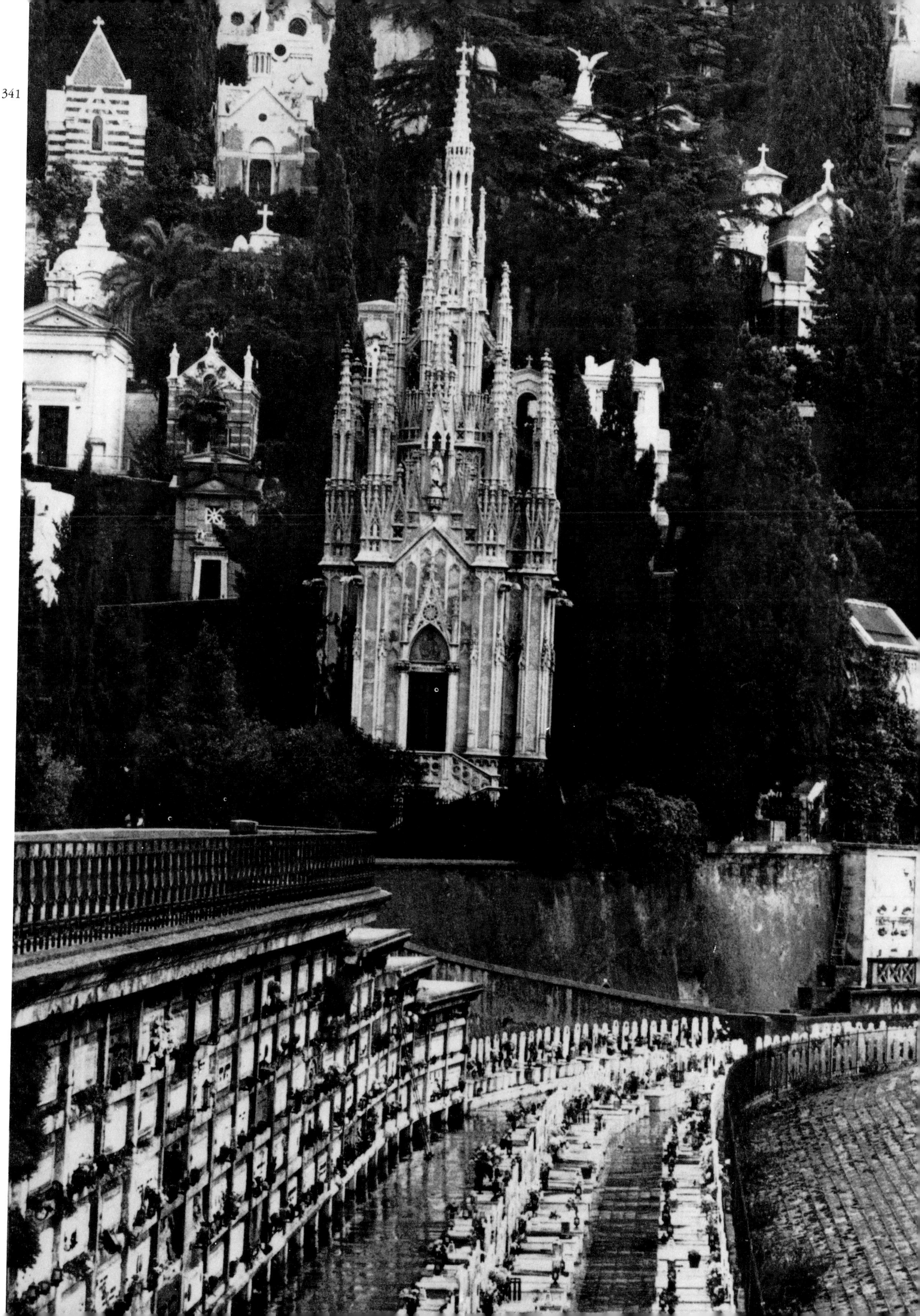

342

343

342. Nineteenth-century view of
Père-Lachaise Cemetery. Musée
Carnavalet, Paris.

343. Tombs in Père-Lachaise
Cemetery. Bibliothèque Nationale,
Paris.

344. Mount Auburn Cemetery,
Cambridge, Massachusetts.

candles (332), spades (333) or goldsmith's hammers — the instrument or the products of the subject's labors. These professional symbols may be compared with the ploughs found in the little cemetery in Luxembourg or the cobbler's tools in Lisbon. They are all evidence of an artisan or peasant pride which became noticeable as early as the end of the fifteenth century (one of the many examples is a vine-grower's pruning knife on a large cemetery cross dated 1458; see illustration 334) and in the sixteenth century too, but which developed above all in the eighteenth century. It inspired an original folk-art iconography (which disappeared in the nineteenth century) and also a desire to affirm personal identity, which caused the use of the individual and family tomb (for "so-and-so and his family") and the commemorative monument to spread beyond the church to more modest social levels. Thus, alongside the cemeteries with disk-shaped or vertical stelae, there appeared in the eighteenth century a third type of cemetery whose structural element was the horizontal tombstone.

The correspondence between the tombstone and the body

At the end of the eighteenth century, despite the growing practice of burying the dead inside churches, outdoor cemeteries were no longer empty spaces: they were beginning to be colonized by modest funerary monuments. Eventually, during the first half of the nineteenth century, in France, the three elements (crosses, vertical stelae, and horizontal tombstones), hitherto used separately, were combined to constitute a single type of extremely common tomb, such as can be seen in Marville (335): the inscription appears on the vertical stela, as was customary; the horizontal stone is decorated with a cross flanked by two chandeliers, symbolizing light; the vertical stela is surmounted by another cross.

This design stemmed from the fact that the tomb was now required not only to mark the location of the burial place but also — and this was a new preoccupation — to cover it exactly. As J.-D. Urbain has pointed out, the tomb became a substitute for the body and had to reproduce its dimensions. That is why, in France, a tombstone copied from the funerary stones of churches and cloisters would be placed in front of the stela, which long retained its epigraphic function. In England, a little footstone would be placed over the feet of the deceased, the vertical stela remaining in position as a headstone.

Beginning in the nineteenth century, the body and the tomb were required to coincide. It was no longer considered acceptable to pile corpses one on top of another, as had been customary ever since the *ad sanctos* burials. Nor would moving them to charnel houses — where they would be dispersed, skulls on one side, long bones on the other — be tolerated any longer. However, this development did not come about all at once. There were a number of interim compromises.

The "skullbox" (336) was one way of getting around the anonymity of the charnel house without upsetting customary inhumation practices, until the desire for some individual monument, however humble, became general. The skullbox was a little personal charnel house in which the skull would be deposited and could be *seen* through an opening: "Here lies the head of so-and-so; pray for him." The fact is that, in many places, prayers for the souls in purgatory were associated with contemplation of the skull. In Naples, each of the faithful chooses a skull from the charnel-house heap; he or she then prays for that soul and thus speeds it on its way to paradise. The practice of displaying the

236

skull is connected with devotions such as these. In Marville, skullboxes appeared alongside the old charnel houses of medieval origin in the early nineteenth century (337), only to be themselves abandoned in favor of the individual and definitive tomb.

At the end of the eighteenth century, things began to change. The whole idea of the cemetery was called into question. Enlightened minds condemned the unhealthy aspects of common graves and large charnel houses situated in the middle of towns. There were many ideas about the form that the cemetery of the ideal city should take. There was much debate and many plans were put forward, some of them — those of Jomard, for instance (338) — futuristic and surrealistic.

A curious little semicircular mock window in the Vatican Library represents a view of the *campo santo* of the Hospital of the Santo Spirito in Rome (339). I would be surprised if this were an accurate representation of reality and not a rearrangement of it — that is, an image of how the famous hospital's cemetery *ought* to have been. It shows a geometric space consisting of rows of plain horizontal stones, all identical. People walk around it, but there are places to pray on the right and the left, marked by large bas-reliefs resembling altarpieces.

In my view, this is a religious model of the ideal cemetery, inspired by the Christian tradition. It is curious to find in the alignment of the stones an echo of fifteenth-century resurrection scenes, which were themselves probably derived from the theatrical settings of Mystery plays.

345. View of Greenwood Cemetery, Brooklyn, New York, by James Smillie (1847). Collection of Donald E. Simon.

The displacement of cemeteries in the nineteenth century

346. Aerial view of the cemetery of Toulouse.

In the course of the nineteenth century, the old cemeteries around the churches disappeared. This was an important turning point. In Chapter 1, we saw how tombs entered the towns. Now they moved out again. Public administrators decided to have them set at a distance, as in Graeco-Roman times. This was a fascinating and complicated development that reveals a whole new side of the contemporary sensibility.

The displacement of the cemeteries, in conjunction with the new desire for individual, definitive tombs at the actual place of burial, obliged town planners to devise an entirely new cemetery model.

In England, characteristically, the municipal authorities were unable to act, and the new style of cemetery was provided by capitalism.

In Italy and other Mediterranean countries, attempts were made to remain faithful to the traditional idea of the cloister with arcades (340); but however large the cloisters were made, they could not contain the great invasion of tombs, and plans for adequate extensions were not always made. Possibly that is why, after a while, a new solution was adopted: that of accommodating the tombs one above another, with the recesses opening as in a chest of drawers (341).

I cannot help wondering whether this practice—found in Italy, Spain, Portugal, and Latin America—did not originate from a disinclination to abandon the traditional plan of the cloister, despite its being so ill-suited to urbanization and to new funerary practices.

Apart from Mediterranean regions and those of Iberian cultures, western Europe and North America adopted a new type of cemetery, early nineteenth-century models of which are Père Lachaise (342, 343) and Montparnasse Cemetery in Paris, Highgate in London, and Mount Auburn Cemetery in Massachusetts (344). Contemporary photographs and, even better, engravings make it possible to understand the effect aimed for and appreciate the extent to which this conception of the cemetery differed from, say, that of Les Innocents.

The new cemetery was located outside the town, in a picturesque spot. It was designed as a park, a public garden, offering a welcome to the stroller. It was also a sort of museum of the famous, a pantheon where national heroes were honored. The tombs were scattered over the grass. The concept of death that emerged was altogether new, less linked to religion and more associated with both public and private life. The bereaved adopted a habit they had never had before—that of regularly visiting the tombs of those whom death had wrested from them. Nature's hospitality would assuage their grief (345).

Since the nineteenth century, that model has not altered; however, it has proved impossible to preserve its aesthetic qualities, and in many cases the cemetery-parks have lost their green spaces. As soon as the expanding towns took them over, they became completely filled with tombs. These new cemeteries were put together like huge, rapidly overpopulated allotments. The aerial photograph of the cemetery of Toulouse (346) shows the extent to which the urban fabric has been eroded by these huge necropolises.

347

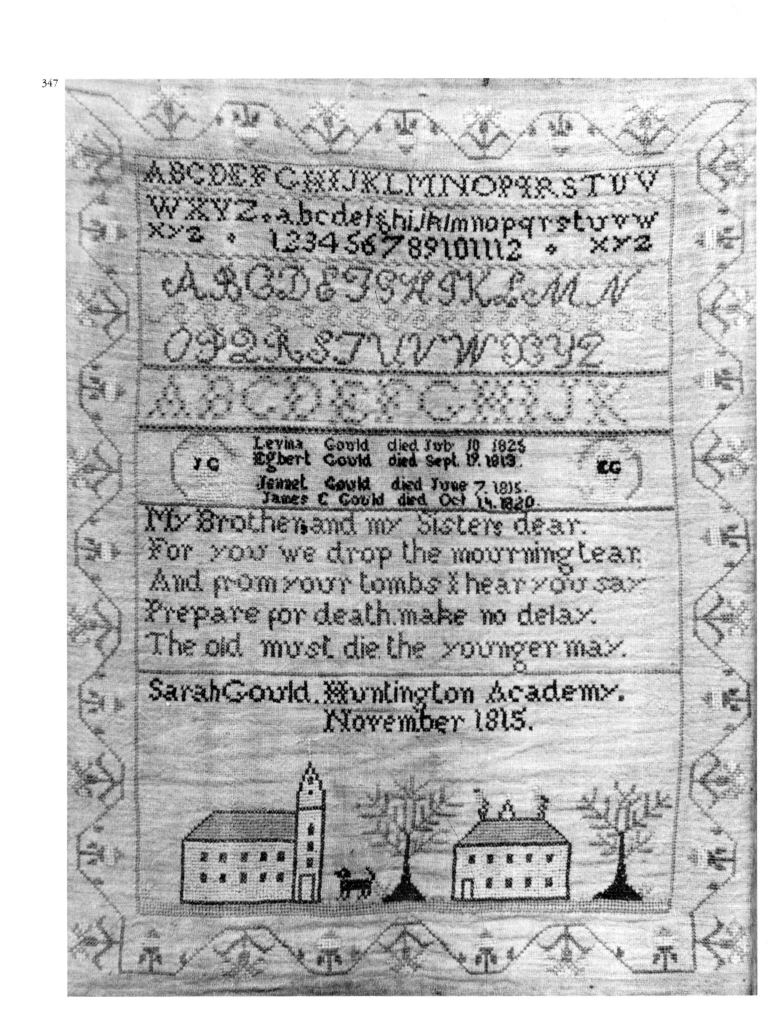

7. The death of others

In the nineteenth century everything changed. Initially, death had been restricted to a few specific places. When it had exceeded those boundaries, beginning in the sixteenth century, it had simply taken for its own the subterranean expanses of the imaginary, without emerging at the surface of daily life. But now daily life was never free of death, for death was everywhere present and cultivated. The fashion was not to fear it, but to live gladly in its presence.

All this emerges quite clearly from the first image in our new series. It is a very ordinary piece of evidence, an end-of-year task such as all American girls of the early nineteenth century used to produce (347). Such a sampler, in which a girl would display her manual dexterity and express an idea or sentiment close to her heart, was usually a reflection of family or religious piety. She would then keep the piece of work in her home throughout her life, hanging it on the wall of her bedroom or living room, a souvenir of the childhood to which she wished to remain faithful.

Sarah Gould's embroidery dates from 1815. It starts, as was customary, with the letters of the alphabet rendered in several styles, together with a string of arabic numerals, indications of the original utilitarian and pedagogical purpose of the exercise. It continues with a brief composition of a more personal nature: a memorial bearing the names of a brother, Egbert, and a sister, Jannet, the former having died in 1813, the latter in June 1815, only a few months before the completion of the sampler. Death would often strike children; but people were no longer resigned to that fact, and the memory of dead children would be cultivated with an intensity as great as the grief provoked by their passing.

To these names and initials, little Sarah added an epitaph: its words had no doubt been suggested to her by adults at home or at school, but its sentiments doubtless had ample time to make a heartfelt impression, with every stitch of the needle: "My brothers and my sisters dear, / For you we drop the mourning tear / And from your tombs I hear you say: / Prepare for death, make no delay. / The old must die, the younger may."

The traditional *memento mori* is here no longer merely a pious cliché. In the older form of epitaph, a stranger would address the random passer-by; but here, siblings are speaking to their own sister.

At the bottom of her sampler, Sarah embroidered a naïve picture of the scenes of her youth—the house, the orchard, the dog, and the church near which the dear departed were buried.

From our own, contemporary point of view, it is surprising that a little girl should devote her school-year task to the memory of a brother and sister and to the uncertainty of death. Today, we do not consider such themes suitable for children. But there was more to come. Sarah returned home, the years passed, and death struck twice more: first in 1820, then again in 1825. On each occasion Sarah took the mourning embroidery (as it was called) down from the wall and added a new name to the ones already there. She was also obliged to tack on to the words "brother" and "sister" a couple of *s*'s—rather clumsy ones, on account of the lack of space.

Her additions reveal the place that this portable and domestic memorial held in the sensibility of the age: the adult did not forget the work of

347. Cross-stitch sampler by Sarah Gould (1815). Huntington Historical Society, New York.

348. Lithograph memorial, with space left for name and dates. Private collection.

348

349

349. E. Friant, *Grief* (late nineteenth century). Musée Carnavalet, Paris.

350. *Memento mori* of ebony and ivory (eighteenth century). The Museums at Stony Brook, New York, gift of E. Hayden.

351. Statue of praying widow in the cemetery of Nice.

352. Memorial pendant, dated 1780. Victoria and Albert Museum, London.

353. Bracelet clasp, dated 1790. Eleutherian Mills Historical Library, Greenville, Delaware.

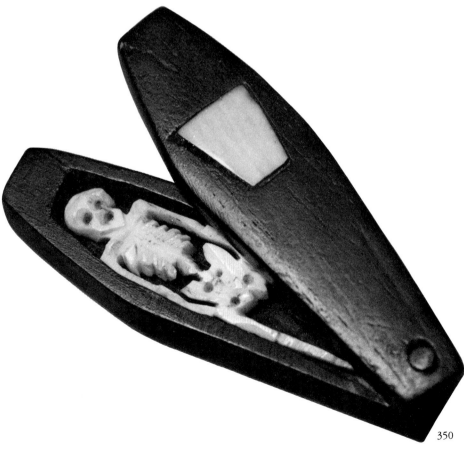

350

351

352

353

the child she had been and took pains to keep it up to date, thus living always with the carefully nurtured memory of the beloved dead.

There were also "mourning pictures" — mass-produced lithographs in which a space would be left for the inscription and names, so that the bereaved could fill these in by hand (348).

In the nineteenth century, death, as revealed by these documents, did not mean one's own fearful and uncertain death, stealing up unawares, but the death that carried off loved ones: the death of others.

Death was so ubiquitous in the nineteenth and early twentieth centuries because it represented both a real separation, which one appropriately mourned with tears testifying to one's stricken love, and also an appearance from which the residue of reality had to be expelled so that communications with the departed could be reestablished.

Hence, the principal funerary customs of the period: exaggerated expressions of grief, cults of memory, and frequent visits to cemeteries and tombs.

Illustration 349 gives a good idea of the manifestations that mourning might take: latter-day versions of the *mater dolorosa,* veiled in black from head to foot, express their feelings with exaggerated and pathetic gestures. Good taste demanded that people seem physically incapable of tolerating the separation from the deceased; and in most cases they did not need to force themselves — they would spontaneously behave as expected. Consider, for example, illustration 351, which shows a widow praying on her husband's tomb.

Beginning in the eighteenth century, the *memento mori* that had previously been objects of piety (279) became mourning lockets. Their

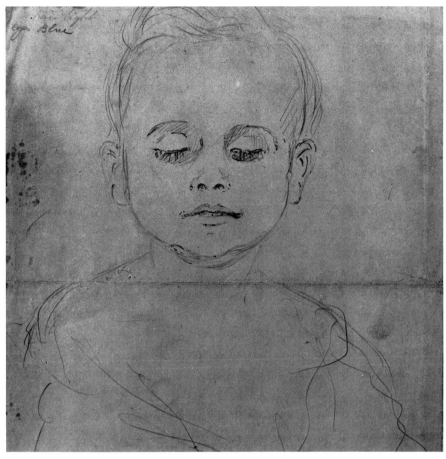

357. Charles Wilson Peale, *Rachel Weeping* (1772–1776). Philadelphia Museum of Art, Barra Foundation collection.

358. Daguerreotype attributed to V. A. Latapié (nineteenth century). Collection of Gilbert Gimon.

359. Portrait of a dead child (c. 1900). Léger-Cabaret collection.

360. Daguerreotype (c. 1852) by Maria Chambefort, Roanne. Collection of Gilbert Gimon.

354. William Sidney Mount, *Portrait of a Woman after Her Death* (nineteenth century). The Museums at Stony Brook, New York, gift of W. Melville.

355. Shepard Alonzo Mount, *Portrait of Camille* (1868). The Museums at Stony Brook, New York.

356. Photographic portrait on enamel, by Alophe (1875). Collection of Gilbert Gimon.

357

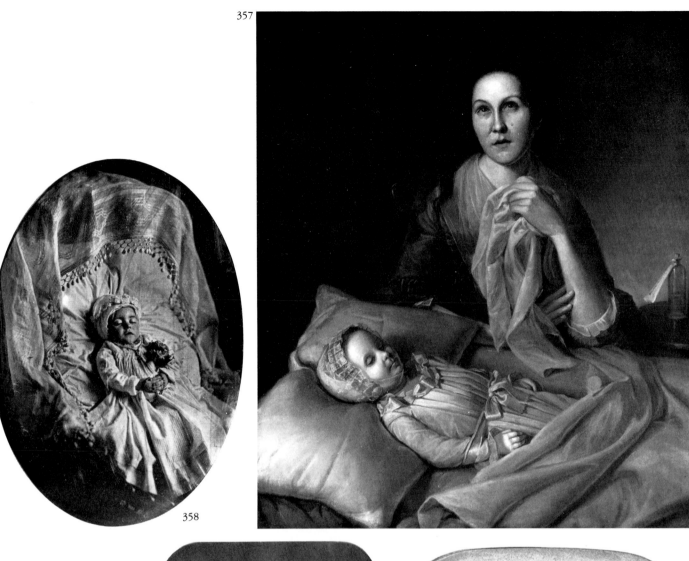

358

359

360

purpose was not so much to help prepare the wearer for death, but to perpetuate the memory of the deceased (350). Some bore reproductions of the loved one's tomb (352), with his or her initials, name, or portrait (VII). Others held a lock of hair — in other words, a fragment of the body.

The mourning locket associated the symbolism of grief (black stones) with an evocation of a presence. Belief in an afterlife did not eclipse death but, on the contrary, contributed to its exaltation: the primary memory to be fixed and perpetuated was that of the individual in death, not in life. Sarah Gould did not embroider the dates of her siblings' births, only those of their deaths. People turned to art for images of the deathbed. The American painters W. S. and S. A. Mount specialized in portraits of the dead (354, 355). The subjects were rendered with closed eyes, as they appeared when laid out on display after their last toilette: there can be no mistaking that they are dead. Later on, paintings were replaced by photographs, which were even more realistic (356). There seems to be a revival here of the seventeenth-century paintings discussed earlier (293 – 296); perhaps in America there was an unbroken tradition of such images.

One senses a determination to preserve at all costs the memory of the *moment of death.* An extreme example is the extraordinary American painting shown in plate VIII, in which the living — the father clasping his head in his hands, the faithful servant praying, and the little boy, attentive but terrified — surround a group of three dead figures: seated in the kind of chair that used to be used for childbirth is the mother, already in the grip of rigor mortis, head thrown back, eyes not yet closed, and hands awkwardly clasped; on her knees are the two dead children that have just emerged from her womb, their eyes wide open like their mother's.

Children were the first beneficiaries of this new desire for preservation — at least by means of imagery and memory — which became defined at the end of the eighteenth century and reached its climax in the mid-nineteenth, particularly in the funerary statues of cemeteries.

In the early days, the images would show a weeping mother at her child's bedside, as in illustration 357. The painter, Charles Wilson Peale (1741 – 1827), entitled this fine portrait *Rachel Weeping,* as if the mother's grief were in need of a biblical precedent. In later images, the child was represented alone on its deathbed, just like an adult, clasping a rosary (358).

In the second half of the nineteenth century, photography superseded painting and endowed the theme with extraordinary popularity. Few family albums were without their photographs of dead children. But a closer look reveals that the body was presented in a new and different pose: no longer a little corpse, it was arrayed in its Sunday best, seated in an armchair, and (as we have already noted in previous illustrations) shown with its eyes partly or completely open. In the case of the photographs, it may be that the eyes had not been closed in time; but children were depicted the same way in paintings (361) and sculptures (362), so the open eyes could not have been a result of chance or clumsiness. Rather, the pose was a response to the need to display children — unlike adults — as alive rather than dead. The deaths of children were the first deaths that could not be tolerated. Prior to the fifteenth century, childrens' tombs either did not exist or were very

Plates VII and VIII: following page 96.

361. Charles Cottet, *The Dead Child.* Bibliothèque des Arts Décoratifs, Paris.

362. Tomb of a Child in Montparnasse Cemetery, Paris.

363

364

363. Funerary sculpture in Staglieno Cemetery, Genoa.

364. Advertisement for a shop selling mourning articles (c. 1900). Eleutherian Mills Historical Library, Greenville, Delaware.

365. Advertisement for an undertaker's establishment (nineteenth century). Eleutherian Mills Historical Library, Greenville, Delaware.

366. Tomb of Luigi Pastorini (1902), by G. Navarone. Staglieno Cemetery, Genoa.

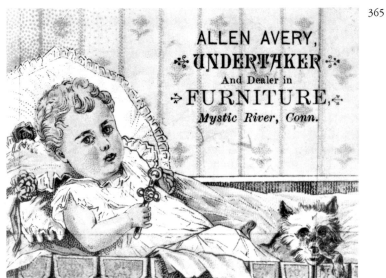

365

367. Tomb of a child in Staglieno Cemetery, Genoa.

368. Tomb of Enrico Amerigo (1890), by G. Moreno. Staglieno Cemetery, Genoa.

369. Tomb of a child in Passy Cemetery, Paris.

370. Tomb dated 1886 in the Jewish cemetery of Milan.

371. Tomb of a child in Loctudy Cemetery, Finistère.

372. Tomb of a baby in Mount Auburn Cemetery, Cambridge, Massachusetts.

370

371

372

373. Tomb of a boy in the cemetery of Milan.

374. Tomb of the Cornetti sisters in the cemetery of Nice.

rare. In the seventeenth century, they were still rare and crude. But in the nineteenth century, the cemeteries were taken over by children. Parents evidently desired to represent their dead children in all kinds of attitudes in order to express their intense grief and their passionate desire to make their children survive in memory and in art, to exalt the children's innocence, charm, and beauty. That is why undertakers — in the United States, at least — felt no qualms about using children in their advertisements (364, 365). After all, children were their best clients.

In Italian funerary sculpture the settings are sometimes dramatic, as in the example of the nursing nun offering to God the body of her suffering little patient (366) or that of the boy indicating heaven to his kneeling sister (363). Sometimes the children are caught at the moment of their mysterious entry into the beyond: a little girl, deep in reverie, raises her eyes to heaven (367); another makes the sign of the cross (368); a third lies on her deathbed with her eyes still open, as an angel prepares to cover her with a fine embroidered sheet (370).

In France, a simpler presentation was preferred, such as a lifelike portrait of the dead child (369, 371). In the United States a symbol would often suffice — a cradle, for example (372).

Adolescents soon came to share with children the privileges that resulted from the refusal to accept their deaths. The sculptor would imagine them either full of life and vitality (373) or at the moment of their passing into immortality. In Nice (374) two young sisters step forward into the beyond, with their hands full of flowers (often symbols of immortality in this iconography); they gaze straight ahead like the somber, melancholy figures found on fourth-century Hellenistic stelae. On another tomb, two disembodied young girls float heavenward together (375).

In this way, the tombs of the new cemeteries of the nineteenth century outdid their Baroque predecessors of the sixteenth century in pathos and imagination. They offer countless examples of expressive portraits and theatrical compositions.

The first actors in these funerary dramas were children or adolescents, in many cases accompanied by their mothers. But before long, the whole family would gather at the place of burial. On a bas-relief in Venice (376) which is slightly reminiscent of Greek funerary art, a dead girl walks down a flight of steps without turning back, cradling a bouquet of the flowers of immortality. Her father and her dog calmly watch her go; behind them an elderly woman — no doubt deceased — barely emerges from the background. This is a family reunion of the living and the dead in which no one, not even the dog, has been forgotten. Such anecdotal art is so personal that in order to interpret it correctly, one really needs to know the story behind each image. What can be the significance of the family gathering in illustration 379, in which two men who look like twins stand quietly behind the chair of a severe-looking woman wearing a little cross around her neck? There is nothing here to suggest death or the cruelty of separation.

The iconography of this period reveals two major currents.

One peacefully turns its back on death and presents gatherings like those seen in Dutch paintings of the seventeenth century — gatherings that might well have been occasioned by an ordinary family celebration, if not some administrative council (see 379).

The other current concentrates on the moment of death — a moment in which sentiments devalued in the course of daily life regain their

375. Tomb of two sisters in the cemetery of Nice.

376. Tomb of the Palnello family, by A. de Lotto (nineteenth century). Cemetery of Venice.

375

376

377. Funerary sculpture in the cemetery of Nice.

intensity and immediacy, and seek emotional expression. For this reason, the moment of death is a favorite subject of salon paintings as well as funerary sculpture.

In plate IX a young woman has just died. The gray angel of death hovers over the scene in the form of a statuette affixed to the wall, lending a symbolic significance to the scene. The dead woman is stretched out on her bed, and her husband embraces her passionately —a last, impossible farewell. This American scene is found in almost identical form on Italian tombs; in illustration 378, it is the young wife who bends over the deathbed of her husband.

Whether young or old, the spouse who is left behind (and who is often past the prime of life) cannot allow the loved one to depart without a final kiss. It was considered important to reproduce on the tomb the wrenching moment just prior to the transferral of the body to the coffin, when the beloved face, still recognizable and stamped with the appearance of life, is about to disappear forever. In fact, life has already fled: in illustration 377, the arm that hangs from the bed is already that of a dead woman.

Plate IX: following page 96.

254

378

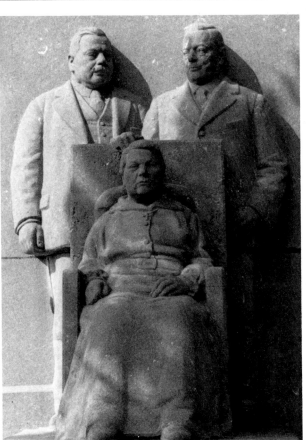

379

378. Tomb of Raffaele Pienovi
(1879), by G. B. Villa. Staglieno
Cemetery, Genoa.

379. Funerary sculpture in the
cemetery of Nice.

255

380. Tomb of Carlo Raggio (1872),
by A. Rivalta. Staglieno Cemetery,
Genoa.

381. Funerary sculpture in the
cemetery of Nice.

382. Tomb of F. G. Casella (1884),
by G. Benetti. Staglieno Cemetery,
Genoa.

383a

383b

383a and 383b. The famous tomb of
the Fournier family. Loix, Île de Ré,
Charente-Maritime.

In other cases, the despairing tête-à-tête between husband and wife gives way to a farewell from the entire family, young and old alike. In a famous and often reproduced scene from Genoa (380), daughters, sons, and all await the last sigh of their elderly father.

There are other ways, too, of representing the continuity of the generations and reconstituting the unity of the family despite the interruption of death. A widow comes to the cemetery and lifts her son up to the portrait of the deceased, which the child, deceived by the likeness and by his own love, is about to embrace as he would his living father (382).

These scenes were common in the south, in Italy or Nice. In Paris, such realistic settings were usually avoided. A more discreet though no less pathetic and significant symbolism was preferred.

In illustration 381 a young woman kneels before the portraits of her dead parents, gazing at them, demonstrating her desire to preserve their memory.

The cemeteries of the nineteenth century were museums of family love. They represented the myriad questions raised by the deaths of others and the attempts to respond to or come to terms with them. The

384. Another view of the Fournier tomb. Loix, Île de Ré, Charente-Maritime.

385. Clasped hands on a tomb in Ars-en-Ré Cemetery, Île de Ré, Charente-Maritime.

examples I have selected, because they are the finest, obviously come from the tombs of the rich. But there were also more modest ones that conveyed the same message, even if by more modest means.

In the second half of the nineteenth century, there were two categories of ordinary tombs which reflected the beliefs of the middle classes in both the towns and the countryside.

The first, not very common, appeared in localities where there were still craftsmen capable of fulfilling the commissions of the lesser gentry. Such tombs display a naïve, unambitious kind of art. I know of a number of examples, the best-known of which is the tomb of the Fournier family in Île de Ré, called *le célèbre tombeau*—"the famous tomb" (383a, 383b, 384). It assembles the entire family in statue form around the father, who is in the middle with his arms crossed, holding a pencil and a notebook. There are many examples showing spouses with clasped hands (385), united in death as in life. Other tombs display personal or original designs either chosen by the family or resulting from the inspiration of some independent workshop—as, for example, a tomb dating from 1931 on which the bereaved have reproduced the house that the deceased had always wanted (386): "his dream come true" *(tout son rêve)*. Similarly, in Lorraine, where local craftsmen continued to work, the models of academic sculpture were interpreted with a clumsy relish reminiscent of early primitives (387, 388, 389). It cannot be denied that today these popular workshops are disappearing. Virtually everywhere throughout France and continental Europe, commercial production is winning out, imposing its own mass-produced models.

Even so, thanks to the photograph, individual families have spontaneously found a means of imparting warmth to otherwise impersonal and unoriginal monuments. In this second and larger category of popular tombs, the photograph has taken the place held in major funerary art by sculpture. It speaks the same language—that of a family presence, a refusal to allow the dead to be forgotten (391, 392).

The inscription plays the same role, but its style has changed since the Middle Ages, as seen in the following epitaphs from a recently opened cemetery near Paris: "No weeping, no tears, but we miss you." "To my husband: He was of the world where all good things come to an end. Like a rose, he lived the space of a single morning. Your big bunny." Expressions such as these cannot but be genuine!

All this funerary rhetoric was not aimed at the unknown passer-by, as the brief medieval epitaph had been. It was addressed to relatives and friends. Beginning in the early nineteenth century, the tomb became a place of family pilgrimage.

Early nineteenth-century American mourning pictures and mourning embroideries similar to Sarah Gould's frequently depicted a tomb —or, in America, a little family cemetery—which surviving relatives would visit (390). The same scene would also be reproduced on personal ornaments (352).

The tomb was the best place for remembering. There, the memory of the deceased and his or her personality would be recalled, and it might happen—illusion or reality?—that the deceased would vouchsafe some reply: a breath of wind, a flash of lightning, or some apparition (393). That was why the tomb would continue to be visited by mourning families (394).

386. Tomb in Auvers-sur-Oise Cemetery, Val-d'Oise.

387. Arnould tomb in Gémonville
Cemetery, Meurthe-et-Moselle.

388. Tomb in Ligny-en-Barrois
Cemetery, Meuse.

389. Tomb in Avril Cemetery,
Meurthe-et-Moselle.

261

390. Amelia Russel Smith, *Mourning Embroidery* (c. 1810). The Museums at Stony Brook, New York.

391

Overleaf:

393. Commemorative picture (c. 1865). Eleutherian Mills Historical Library, Greenville, Delaware.

394. Painting by William Bouguereau (nineteenth century). Bibliothèque des Arts Décoratifs, Paris.

391. Tomb with photographs in Les Batignolles Cemetery, Paris.

392. Tomb with photograph in the cemetery of Nice.

392

8. What of today?

When the image hunter reaches our own decade, he finds himself at a loss, on unfamiliar ground. The abundance of themes and scenes, which has hitherto made choices difficult, seems to have disappeared.

It is true that the major themes consistently present through the ages do still persist, but in a toned down and unoriginal form. There are still some tombs in the style of the early twentieth century, and a few skeletons linger on in works of surrealist and expressionist inspiration; there is really nothing to indicate the great change that is taking place. That is because the change consists precisely in banishing from the sight of the public not only death but, with it, its icon. Relegated to the secret, private space of the home or the anonymity of the hospital, *death no longer makes any sign.*

Illustrations in pious books demonstrate this retreat of the sign. The first editions of *Don Bosco* (395) still show the familiar deathbed scene. In the most recent edition (396), the saint might easily be suffering from no more than a bad cold and be giving some ordinary instructions to two colleagues (although, admittedly, the latter do look rather worried).

Comic strips certainly present death in new and amazing guises, in extraterrestial forms or in science fiction stories of interplanetary conflicts. These are visions of the extraordinary that bear little relation to everyday experience and are perhaps closer to the imaginary world of the baroque period, although as yet without the coherence and meaning of the long series of images of the past.

This reluctance to give death a symbolic representation—a reluctance that is characteristic of a new culture—is an expression of the growing belief that death is nothing (as Robinson and Rousset claimed; see Chapter 3) and that nothingness cannot be represented or imagined.

And yet it can be. The nothingness of death occupies an important place in one of the arts of our own time, which is an art of the image, of the *living* image—namely, the cinema. Unfortunately, within the space of a short chapter it is difficult to convey every aspect of this importance. More generally, there is perhaps an incompatibility between the image that is fixed and printed and the mobile images of the cinema. The latter cannot be reduced to a single shot that can be taken in at a glance and represented at a single moment in time: it is a dynamic image that extends over a whole sequence, which, if edited, would be distorted.

At least, in general that is the case. But a few directors—among them some of the greatest—have successfully adopted a slow tempo bringing them closer to arts that give an illusion of movement, as do those of the baroque period.

In such circumstances it is possible, without cheating, to halt the film at a single image which, though detached, is neither mutilated nor deformed: it preserves its movement within the fixed frame that would in other circumstances check its dynamism.

This is what I have attempted to do with a famous scene from Bergman's *Cries and Whispers* (397). Its popularity is undeniable proof that it expresses something widely and deeply felt. The servant, Anna, a fine girl glowing with health, is so moved by pity that she suddenly decides

395. From *Don Bosco,* by Jijé (1941). Paris, Éditions Dupuis, 1976.

396. From *Don Bosco,* text by Monique Amiel, drawings by Récréo. Paris, Éditions Fleurus, 1977.

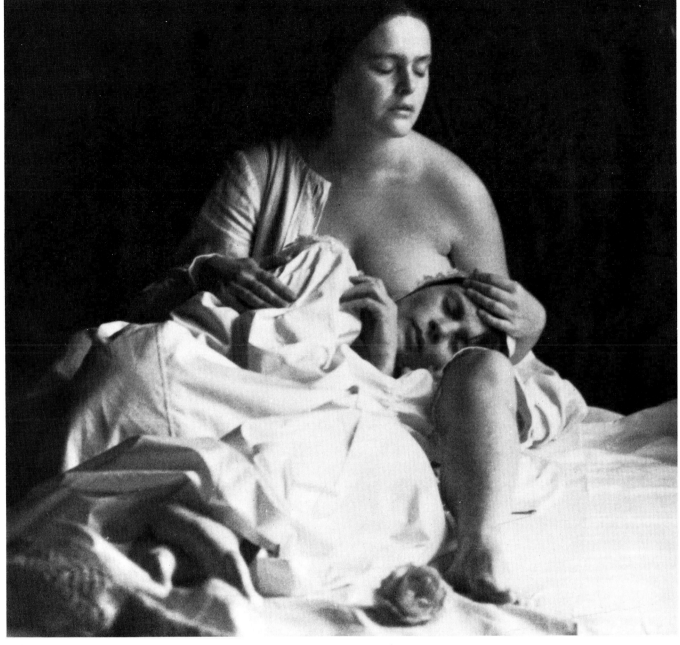

to undress and take her dying mistress in her arms, and, through this
wild embrace which is reminiscent of some primitive witchcraft, to
communicate to her mistress some of the excess of her own vital heat. It
is an extraordinary evocation of the age-old duel between life and
death, and of one possible intercession — that of tenderness and love,
of both the heart and the body.

I suspect that the son of Pastor Bergman was thinking of the passage
in the Book of Kings (IV.4) in which the prophet Elisha brings an
adolescent (*puer*) back to life. He lies down on the dead body, mouth
to mouth, eyes to eyes, hands to hands, glueing himself to the youth and
calling upon the Lord: *incurvavit se super eum*. And soon the young
man's body begins to regain its warmth.

In the film, the scene is inverted, changing its meaning and purpose.
In the first place, it is the adolescent, not the old prophet, who is the
bearer of life and decides to transmit it. Second, in the scene in the film,
there is no longer any God: God is replaced by something which is not

397. A scene from *Cries and
Whispers* (1972), by Ingmar Bergman.

successful in overcoming death, as Elisha's God did, but which at the same time is not an abstract nothingness: it is a love composed of both pity and tenderness, of vital force and physical urge, of a beauty that concentrates within itself the mysterious powers of nature and reproduction.

It is also possible to detect at the origin of this fantastic and primitive scene a very common gesture in the old ritual of death: a person would die *literally* in somebody's arms. Thus, Madame de Sévigné wrote of her uncle Saint-Aubin: "He came out in a great sweat . . . followed by a gentle sleep, which was only interrupted when Father Marcel, *holding him in his arms,* eventually received his last sigh" (italics added).

These now famous images touch upon a symbolism quite different from that of the customary discourse on a death bottled up, privatized, or shut away—a symbolism that could well be lurking beneath the silences of social practice.

Claude Sautet's film *Les Choses de la Vie* ("The Things of Life," 1970) provides us with another illustration of this symbolism running beneath the surface, although here it is in the context of a different philosophy. In this case the dynamism peculiar to the cinema makes it impossible to cut the film to obtain an isolated image. The film evokes the semiconscious thoughts of a dying man, the victim of a car accident. A few decades earlier, it might have been imagined that his last thought would be of his mother (as is said to have been the case with those who died in World War I) or of the Virgin of the *Ave Maria;* but here, parents, spouse, and children have all faded away. God is dead and His face is absent at the moment when some old-fashioned people might still, as in the past, expect it to be revealed for the first time.

No mother, no wife, no children, no God: there appears now to be nothing at all in the wavering consciousness of the dying man. However, this nothingness is not the pure abstraction of Robinson and Rousset. This nothingness has both time and space.

The dying man sees himself not at the wheel of his car but, like a drowned or drowning man, without despair, indifferent, plunged into waters that do not seem hostile. They bear him up for a moment, like a protective medium in which he can still float and make a few gestures before finally sinking for good and disappearing.

The waters in which he is about to disappear are irresistibly reminiscent of the primordial ocean of the first days of the world and, at the same time, of the protective fluids of the womb. Death is associated with a return to birth, to origins.

Thus, a new symbolism, sometimes glimpsed through the cinema and sometimes inspired by extremely ancient beliefs, appears to be forming tentatively around the modern idea of nothingness. But it is a nothingness which is no longer an abstraction and which, as human consciousness has developed, has acquired the density of a span of time, however short, and *the power of the sign.*

Bibliography

In the French edition of this book, Philippe Ariès referred readers to the full bibliography in his *L'Homme devant la mort* (published in English as *The Hour of Our Death*) and mentioned a few recent publications not included in the earlier work. The following list is made up of those titles together with a number of others that may be of interest to readers. The publisher wishes to thank Nicholas Penny, Keeper of Western Art in the Ashmolean Museum, Oxford, for his help in preparing this list and in clarifying many technical points in the translation.

Adhémar, J. "Les Tombeaux de la collection Gaignières." *Gazette des Beaux-Arts* (Paris) 1 (1974): 343–344.

Butler, Patrick Henry. *On the Memorial Art of Tidewater Virginia.* Baltimore: Johns Hopkins University Press, 1969.

Cambelli, Patrizia, and Paolo Guitto. *Quelle figlie, quelle spose.* Rome: De Luca, 1980.

Camporesi, Piero. *Le Pain sauvage.* Paris: Le Chemin Vert, 1981.

Charles-Picard, J. "Étude sur l'emplacement des tombes des papes du IIIe au Xe siècle." *Mélanges d'archéologie et d'histoire de l'École française de Rome* 81 (1969): 735–782.

Chastel, A. "L'Art et le sentiment de la mort au XVIIe siècle." *Revue du XVIIe siècle* 36–37 (1957): 293.

——— "Le Baroque et la mort." *Troisième congrès international des études humanistes* (Rome, 1955): 33–46.

Christ, Y. *Les Cryptes mérovingiennes de Jouarre.* Paris: Plon, 1961.

Davis, Natalie Zemon. "Holbein's *Pictures of Death* and the Reformation at Lyons." *Studies on the Renaissance* 3 (1956): 97–130.

Dictionnaire d'archéologie chrétienne et de liturgie. Paris: Letouzey, 1907.

Dufour, V. "Le Cimetière des Innocents." In F. Hoffbauer, *Paris à travers les âges,* vol. 2, pt. 1, pp. 1–28. Paris: 1875–1882.

——— *La Danse macabre des Saints-Innocents de Paris.* Paris: 1874.

Etlin, R. A. *Landscapes of Eternity: Funerary Architecture and the Cemetery, 1793–1881.* In *Oppositions* 7 (1976).

Favre, R. *La Mort dans la littérature et la pensée française au siècle des lumières.* Lyon: Presses Universitaires de Lyon, 1978.

French, S. "The Cemetery as Cultural Institution." In D. E. Stannard, ed., *Death in America.* Philadelphia: University of Pennsylvania Press, 1975.

Gannal, F. *Les Cimetières de Paris.* Paris: 1884.

Giesey, R. E. *The Royal Funeral Ceremony in Renaissance France.* Genève: Droz, 1960.

Gillon, E. V. *Victorian Cemetery Art.* New York: Dover, 1972.

Hubert, J. *Les Cryptes de Jouarre.* Quatrième congrès de l'Art du haut Moyen Age. Melun: Imprimerie de la préfecture de Seine-et-Marne, 1952.

Huizinga, J. *The Waning of the Middle Ages.* New York: St. Martin's, 1924.

Lavin, Irving. "Sculptor's 'Last Will and Testament.'" *Bulletin of the Allen Memorial Art Museum* (Oberlin College) 35 (1977–78): 1–2.

Le Goff, Jacques. *La Naissance du purgatoire.* Paris: Gallimard, 1982.

——— *La Civilisation de l'Occident médiéval.* Paris: Arthaud, 1964.

——— "Culture cléricale et traditions folkloriques dans la civilisation mérovingienne." *Annales ESC* (July–August, 1967): 780ff.

Mâle, É. *L'Art religieux du XIIe siècle.* Paris: A. Colin, 1940. Published in English as *Religious Art in France: The Twelfth Century.* Princeton, N.J.: Princeton University Press, 1978.

Mercier, S. *Tableaux de Paris.* Paris, 1789.

Mitford, J. *The American Way of Death.* New York: Simon and Schuster, 1963.

Pincus, L. *Death and the Family.* New York: Vintage Books, 1975.

Robinson, Paul. "Five Models for Dying." Review of *The Hour of Our Death. Psychology Today* 15 (March 1981): 85–91.

Rousset, Bernard. "La Philosophie devant la mort." In L. V. Thomas, B. Rousset, and T. V. Thao, eds., *La Mort aujourd'hui.* Colloquium of Amiens. Paris: Editions Anthropos, 1975.

Sicard, Damien. *La Liturgie de la mort dans l'église latine, des origines à l'époque précarolingienne.* Munster: Aschendorff, 1978.

Spencer, Theodore. *Death and Elizabethan Tragedy.* Cambridge, Mass: Harvard University Press, 1936.

Stannard, D. E. *Death in America.* Philadelphia: University of Pennsylvania Press, 1975.

——— *The Puritan Way of Death.* New York: Oxford University Press, 1977.

Tenenti, A. *Il Senso della morte e l'amore della vita nel Rinascimento.* Turin: Einaudi, 1957.

——— *La Vie et la mort à travers l'art du XVe siècle.* In *Cahiers des Annales,* vol 8. Paris: Armand Colin, 1952.

Thomas, V. *L'Anthropologie de la mort.* Paris: Payot, 1975.

Urbain, Jean-Didier. *La Société de conservation.* Paris: Payot, 1981.

Vovelle, G., and M. Vovelle. *Vision de la mort et l'au-delà en Provence d'après les autels des âmes du Purgatoire.* In *Cahiers des Annales,* vol. 29. Paris: Armand Colin, 1970.

Vovelle, M. *Piété baroque.* Paris: Editions du Seuil, 1978.

——— *Mourir autrefois.* Collection *Archives.* Paris: Gallimard, 1974.

Credits

References are to the illustration numbers.

Aix-en-Provence: CNRS-LAMM, J.-M. Allais 22, G. Démians d'Archimbaud 64, 203, M. Fixot and J.-P. Pelletier 87, C. Hussy 205a, 205b; CNRS – Centre Camille Jullian, Foliot 49. — *Lodève:* Musée Fleury, L. Gigou 311a, 311b. — *Metz:* Service Photographique des Musées 146. — *Nancy:* Éditions du Musée Lorrain 154; Inventaire Général de Lorraine, J. Guillaume 389, M.-F. Jacops 387, 388. — *Paris:* Bibliothèque Nationale 30, 147, 148, 168, 172, 173, 186, 187, 193, 231, 235, 317; Musée Carnavalet 13 (photo courtesy of the Musée Archéologique de Laon), 17, 18, 19, 23, 24, 202, 309, 310, E. Michot 29, A. Rivière 206; Musée de l'Homme, C. Lassalle 1; Musées Nationaux 53, 304, 305. — *Toulouse:* Atelier Municipal de Photographie 47, 62, 63, 69, 79, 131, 137, 138, 209. — *Amsterdam:* Historical Museum 262; Rijksmuseum 284. — *Bâle:* Kunstmuseum 258, 300. — *West Berlin:* Staatliche Museen Preussischer Kulturbesitz, J. P. Anders 277. — *Bruges:* Musée Memling – CPAS 174. — *Brussels:* Musée d'Art Ancien 257; Musées Royaux des Beaux-Arts 293; Service National des Fouilles 86. — *Geneva:* Bureau Cantonal d'Archéologie, J.-B. Sevette 12, 55. — *London:* Victoria and Albert Museum 279, 352; Tate Gallery 35; British Museum 38; National Gallery 298. — *Stockholm:* Svenska Porträttarkivet National Museum 288. — *Vatican:* Archives Photographiques des Musées 339. — *Vienna:* Kunsthistorisches Museum 285. — *United States:* Eleutherian Mills Historical Library, Greenville (Del.) 194, 353, 364, 365, 393; Huntington Historical Society, New York 347; The Museums at Stony Brook, New York 345, 350, 354, 355, 390, Ken Spencer 328, 344, 372; Museum of Art, Philadelphia, Will Brown 357.

Archivi Alinari 299. — Xavier Barral i Altet 7, 8, 10, 50, 60, 66, 76, 77, 83, 153, 179, 180. — Guy van Belleghem 295. — Jean Bernard 240. — Bernard Biraben 110. — Noëlle de La Blanchardière 242. — Emmanuel Boudot-Lamotte 5, 21, 51, 93. — Christina von Braun 43, 243. — Anne de Brunhoff 165, 340, 341, 363, 366, 367, 368, 370, 373, 376, 382, 383a, 383b, 384, 385, 391. — Bulloz 157, 303. — Patrick Henry Butler 120, 330. — Danièle Calegari 246, 247, 351, 374, 375, 377, 379, 381, 392. — Mme Carbonell-Lamothe 70, 331, 332, 333. — Jean-Loup Charmet 162, 163, 164, 167, 170, 177, 181, 189, 221, 222, 223, 224, 225, 226, 227, 228, 236, 241, 249, 250, 251, 252, 253, 255, 256, 261, 264, 265, 276, 286, 289, 290, 306, 308, 338, 349, 356, 358, 360, 361, 394. — François Chaslin 327, 378, 380, 386. — Jean Dieuzaide 6, 52, 78, 81, 84, 96, 98, 99, 100, 116, 121, 124, 129, 132, 145, 149, 175, 195, 196, 208, 212, 214, 215, 220, 266, 314, 315, 316, 324, 346, 20 (Archives Municipales de Bordeaux). — Marc Durand 40, 41, 42, 88. — Edimedia-Snark 287. — Catherine Furet 94, 269. — Giraudon 58, 61, 72, 92, 97, 119, 127, 128, 130, 158, 161, 184, 197, 213b, 219, 229, 230, 232, 237, 238, 245, 248, 259, 260, 263, 281, 282, 294, 302. — Alinari-Giraudon 89, 91, 126, 291. — Anderson-Giraudon 133, 151, 275, 292. — Brogi-Giraudon 134. — Garanger-Giraudon 211. — Lauros-Giraudon 82, 155, 159, 176, 185, 188, 191, 192, 198, 207, 218, 239, 280, 283, 296, 301, 307. — Roger Humbert 80b. — Michel Langrognet 74, 85, 90, 107, 108, 109, 111, 113, 114, 115, 118, 122, 125, 135, 139, 152a, 152b, 178, 199, 200, 201, 213, 217, 270, 271, 272, 273, 274, 278, 312. — *L'Avant-Scène* (no. 142) 397. — Léger-Cabaret Collection 359. — Private collection 348. — Monique Lemoine 204. — Jacques Mascré 254. — Jean-Robert Masson 27, 28, 31, 32, 33, 34, 36, 37, 44, 45, 46, 56, 59, 67, 68, 73, 75a, 75b, 80a, 101, 104, 106, 117, 123, 140, 141, 142, 143, 144, 150, 182, 183, 210, 233, 234, 267, 318, 325, 326, 335, 336, 337, 371. — José Mattoso 313. — Monique Mayaud 329. — Achille Olivieri 136. — *Paris-Normandie* 11. — Mme Patcher 362, 369. — Orest Ranum 244. — Rapho, Georg Gerster 15. — Roger-Viollet 4, 9, 65, 95, 105, 112, 160, 169, 171, 190. — Alinari-Viollet 2. — Anderson-Viollet 3. — Cap-Roger-Viollet 57. — LL-Roger-Viollet 102, 103. — ND-Roger-Viollet 156, 166. — Jean Roubier 54, 216. — Marcel Schroeder 71, 268, 297, 319, 320, 321, 322, 323, 334. — Archives Seuil 342, 343.

Plates:
I: Jean-Robert Masson. — II: Bibliothèque Municipale, Reims. — III: Jean Vigne. — IV: Thyssen-Bornemisza Collection, Lugano, Switzerland. — V: Jean Bernard. — VI: Edimedia, Snark Archives. — VII: Douglas H. Gordon Collection. — VIII: Campus Martius Museum, Marietta, Ohio. — IX: North Carolina Museum of Art, Raleigh, North Carolina.

Acknowledgments

This book is really a collective work. Jean-Robert Masson and Claude Simion have had either to trace, with great difficulty in some cases, the originals of the documents reproduced or simply cited in my book *L'Homme devant la mort* (Paris: Seuil, 1977) — in English, *The Hour of Our Death* (New York: Knopf, 1980) — or have had to photograph, often under difficult conditions, those which had not previously been photographed. With the assistance of Agnès Mathieu, who is responsible for the layout of this volume, they also brought to my attention documents which in many cases were new to me and which completed and enriched the iconographic series already projected.

I owe a particular debt of gratitude to Patrick Périn, director of the Musée Carnavalet, and to Jan Armstrong, archivist at the Museums of Stony Brook, in Stony Brook, New York. This book also owes much to the advice, conversations, suggestions, writings, and images provided by a great many people, among them François Arné, Noëlle de La Blanchardière, Serge Bonnet, Christina von Braun, Anne de Brunhoff, Mme Carbonelle-Lamothe, André Chastel, Pierre Chaunu, Pavel Chiaya, John Demos, Sophie Deroisin, Marc Durand, Robert Favre, Catherine Furet, Abbé J. Giry, M.-F. Jacops, Michel Langrognet, Benoît Le Roux, the Friends of Marville (M. Intins), José Mattoso, Achille Olivieri, Erwin Panofsky, Jean-Marie Pézé, Jean-Charles Picard, Antoinette Romain-Lenormand, Marcel Schroeder, David Stannard, Alberto Tenenti, and Michel Vovelle. I hope that those whose names do not appear here will forgive me — I have so many creditors!

This book is printed on acid-free paper, and its binding materials
have been chosen for strength and durability.

Library of Congress Cataloging-in-Publication Data

Ariès, Philippe.
  Images of man and death.

  Translation of: Images de l'homme devant la mort.
  Bibliography: p.
  1. Death in art. 2. Death. 3. Sepulchral
monuments. I. Title.
N8217.D5A713 1985   704.9′493069   85-768
ISBN 0-674-44410-8 (alk. paper)

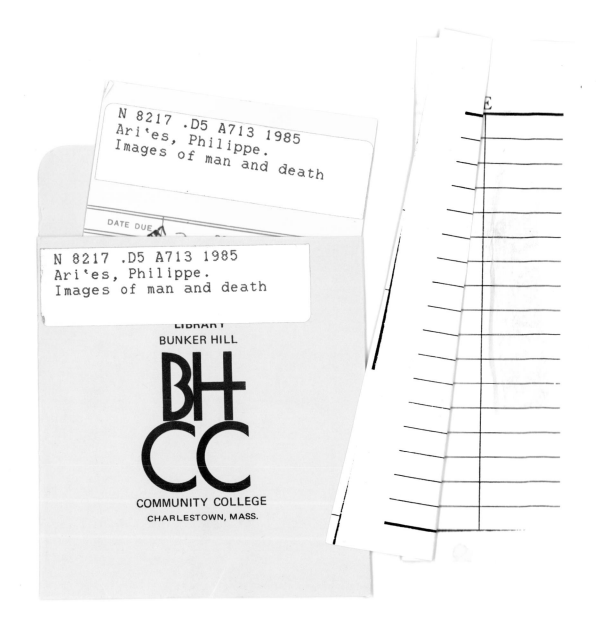

11622286